NAÏVE

MODERNISM AND FOLKLORE IN CONTEMPORARY GRAPHIC DESIGN

gestalten

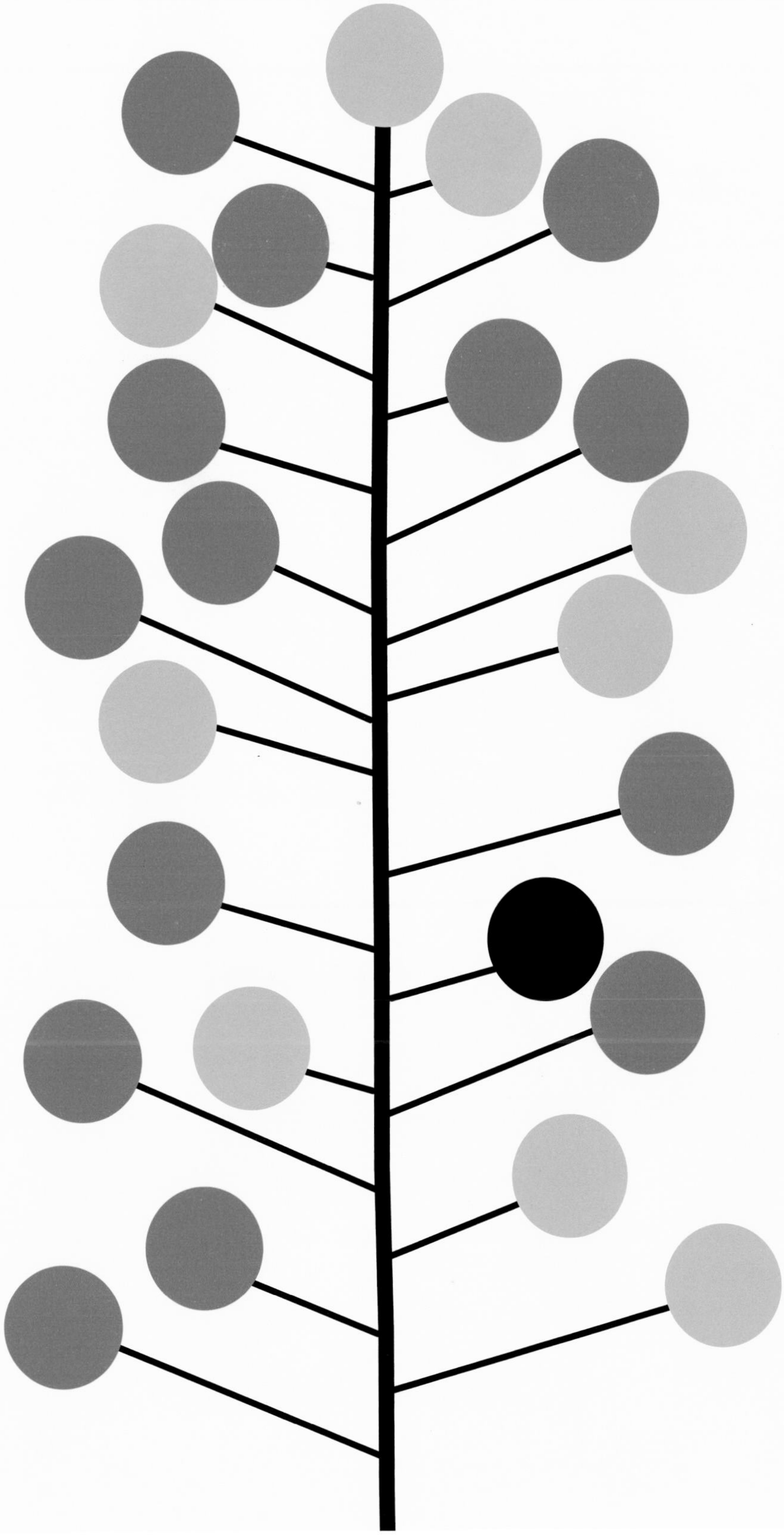

Darling Clementine Haberdashery Series – Personal, 2006

Darling Clementine Candy Cane Christmas Series – Greeting Cards, 2008

Darling Clementine Candy Cane Christmas Series – Greeting Cards, 2008

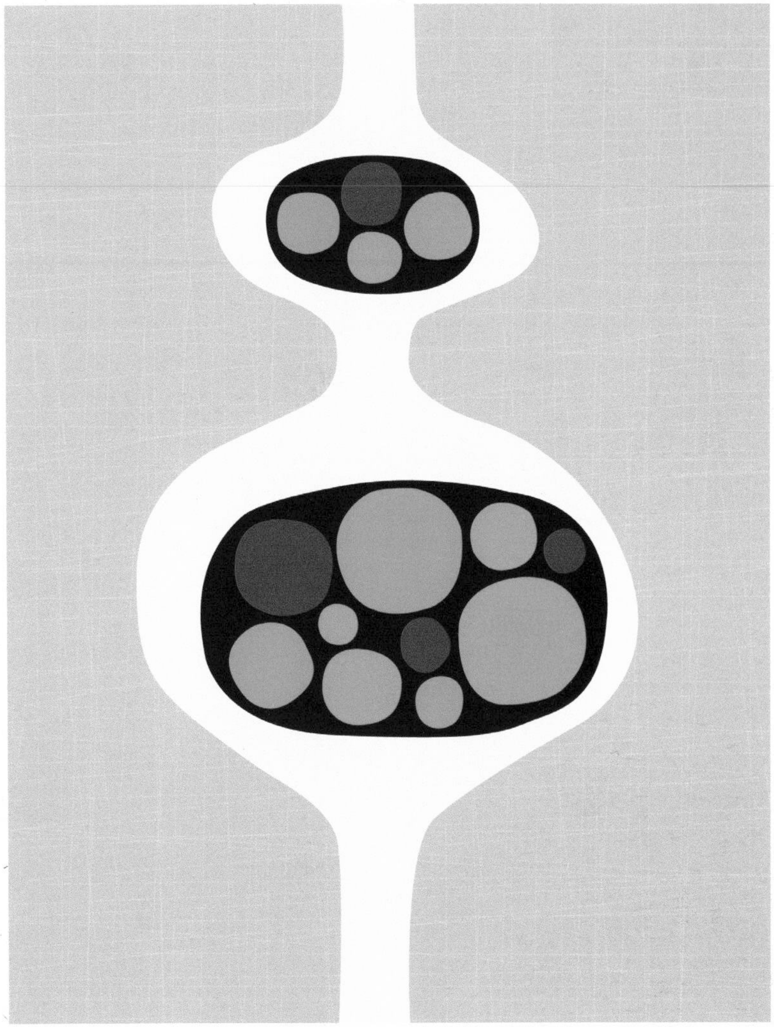

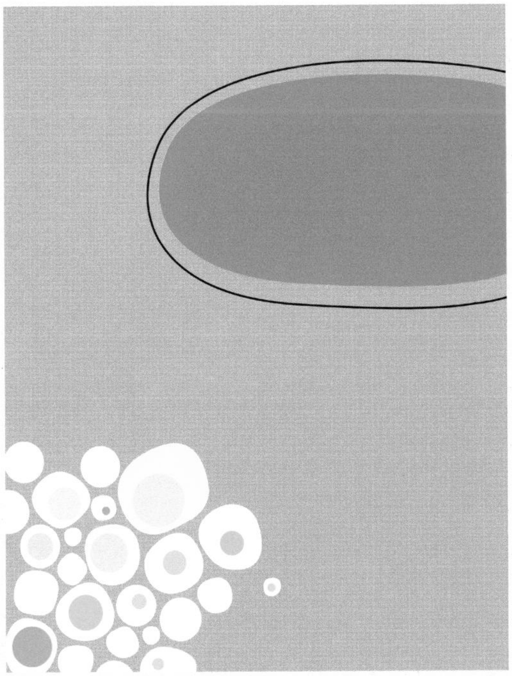

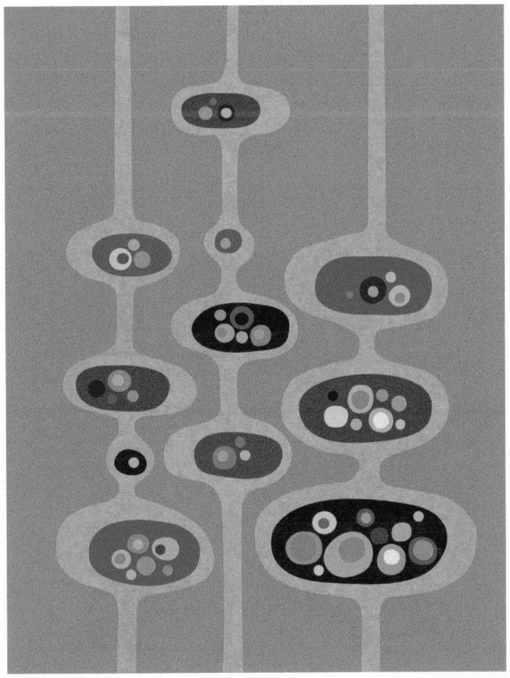

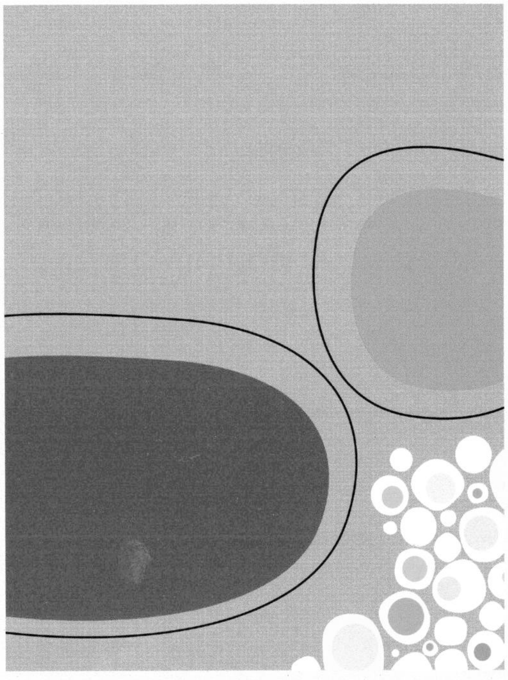

Jenn Ski Diverse – Art Prints, 2007/2008

Lucy Clark Connect 2, Making tracks 1 & 2, Sliced, Mini Chess, Caged – Textile Design, 2007

Lucy Clark Disco – Textile Design, 2007

Jenn Ski Diverse - Art Prints, 2007

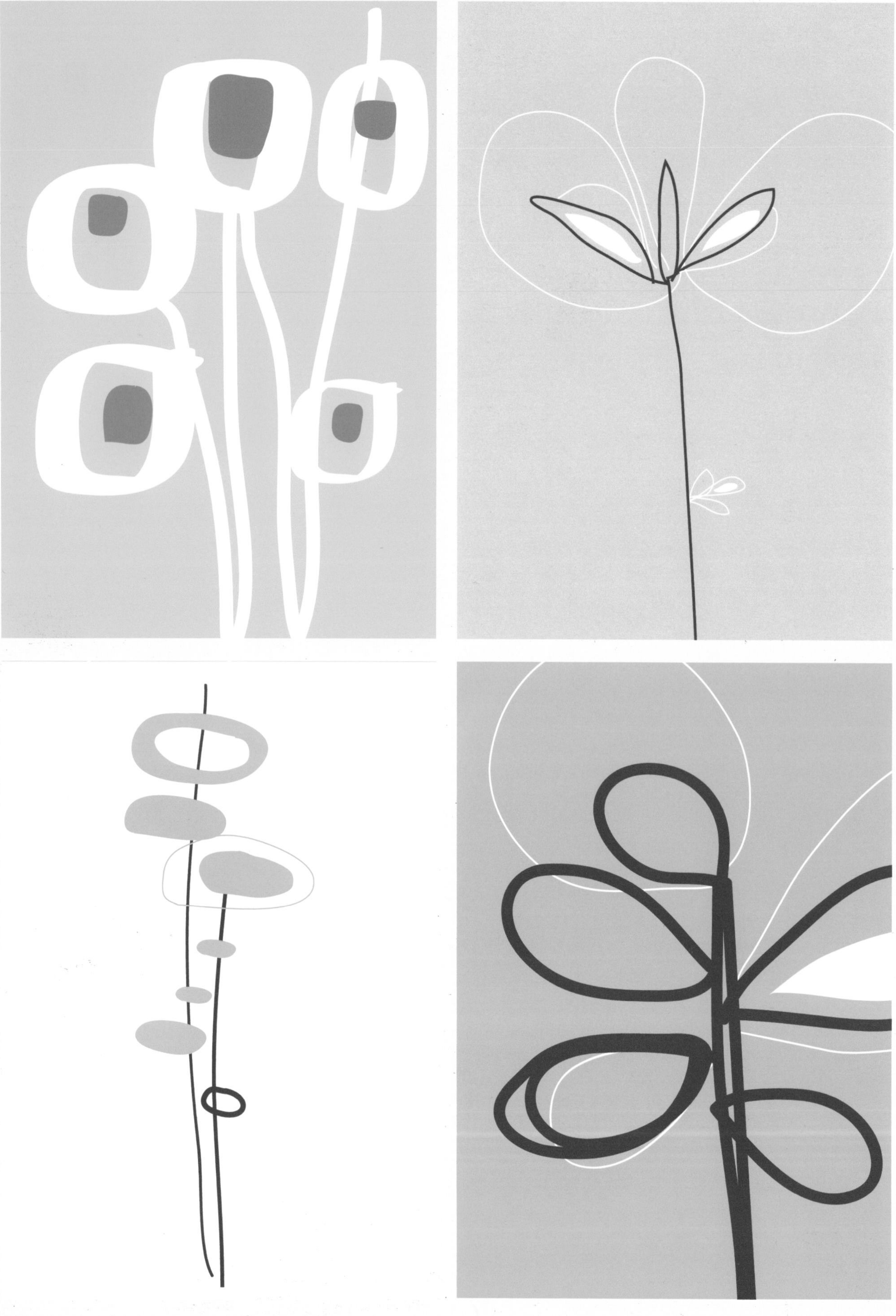

Lexie Sullivan Diverse – Stationery, 2008

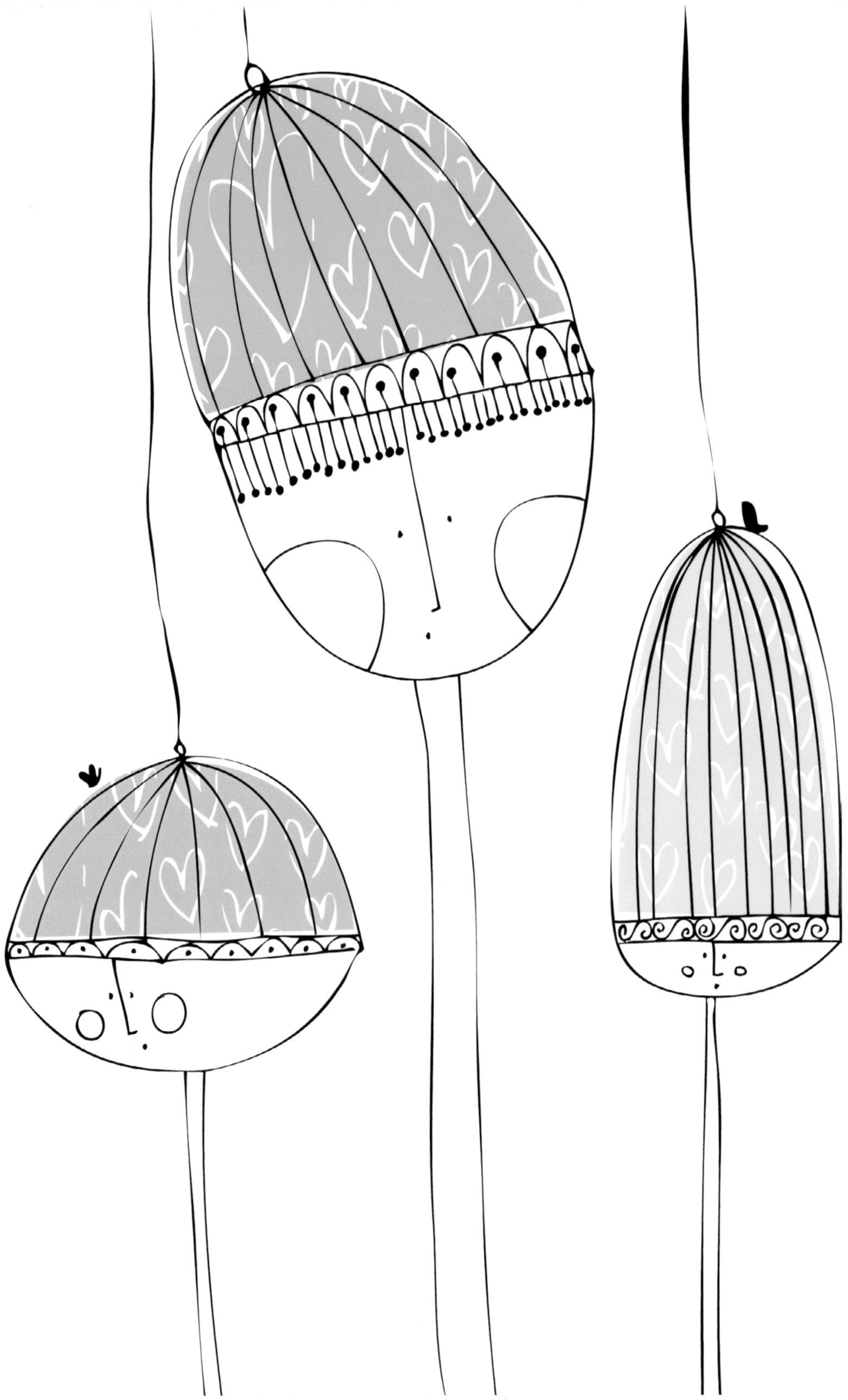

Rülõ Caged-Ones - Poster, 2009

Rülõ Diverse - Notebook Covers. 2008

Darling Clementine Nöel Series – Greeting Cards, 2007

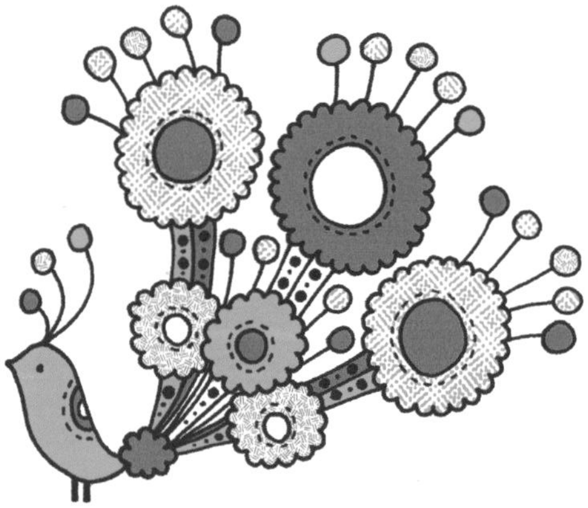

Jen Skelley Puffer Tail (top), Sprout (left), Broccolini (right) - Art Prints, 2008

Nate Duval Hootie (top) - Art Print, 2008 **Jen Skelley** Love Birds (left) - Art Print, 2007 ||| Calendar 2009 (right), 2009

DANCING
TEA
PARK
D
Bubble RooM
CAFE
BAR
DRINK
TEA
Coffee
FUN

Matte Stephens Portland – Painting, 2008

Matte Stephens Boston (top), New Orleans (left), Family Vacation (right) - Paintings, 2008

Dan Stiles Feist, Hot Chip, Ted Leo, Jack Johnson – Posters, 2007/2008

菩提本無樹

何處惹塵埃

本來無一物

明鏡亦非臺

Nod Young The Puti Trees – Personal, 2006

Helen Dardik Mod Friends - Personal, 2007

Helen Dardik Danish Garden Friends - Personal, 2008

HELEN DARDIK

Helen Dardik Bird House Party - Personal, 2009

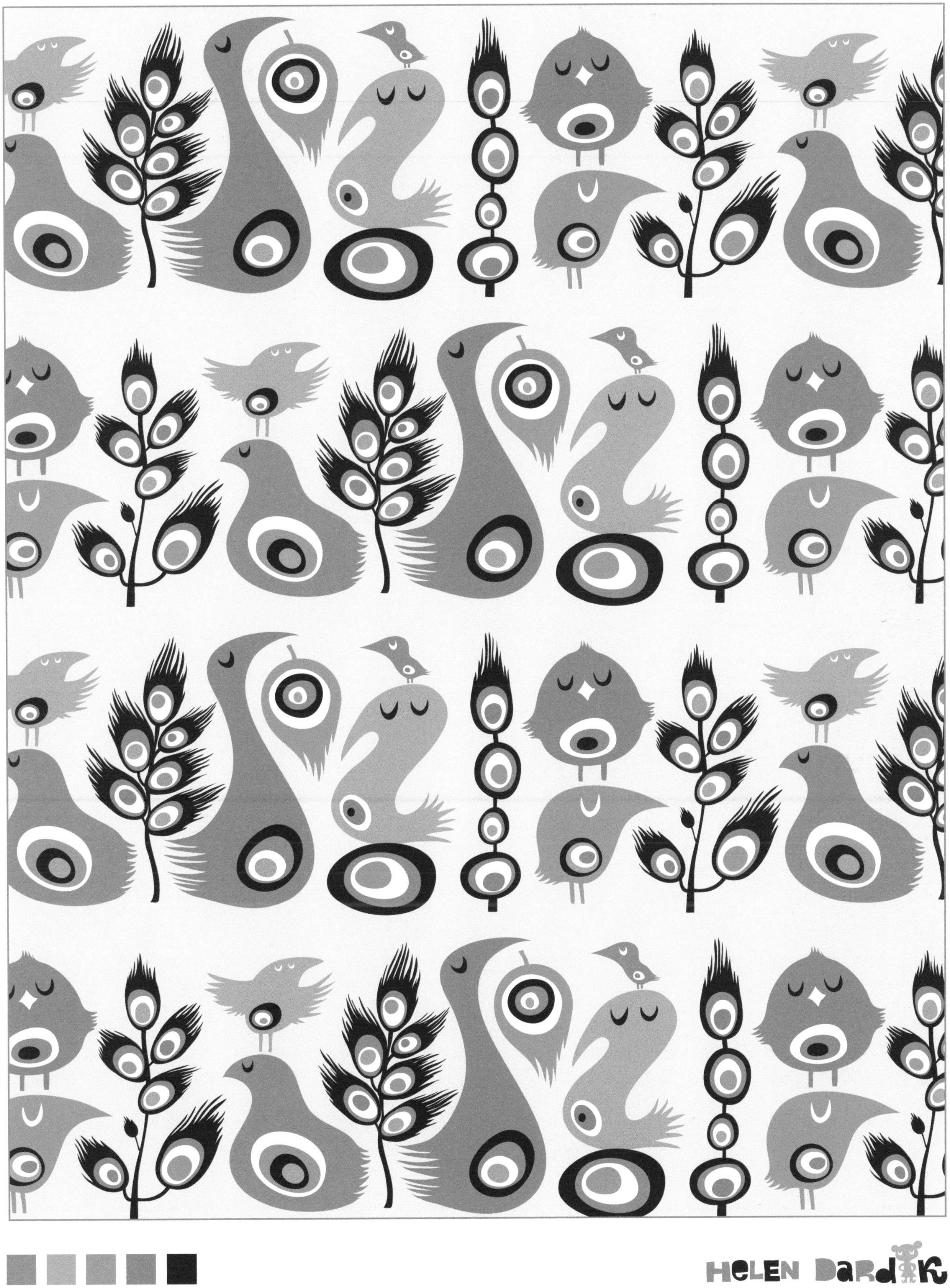

Helen Dardik Bird Parade - Personal, 2008

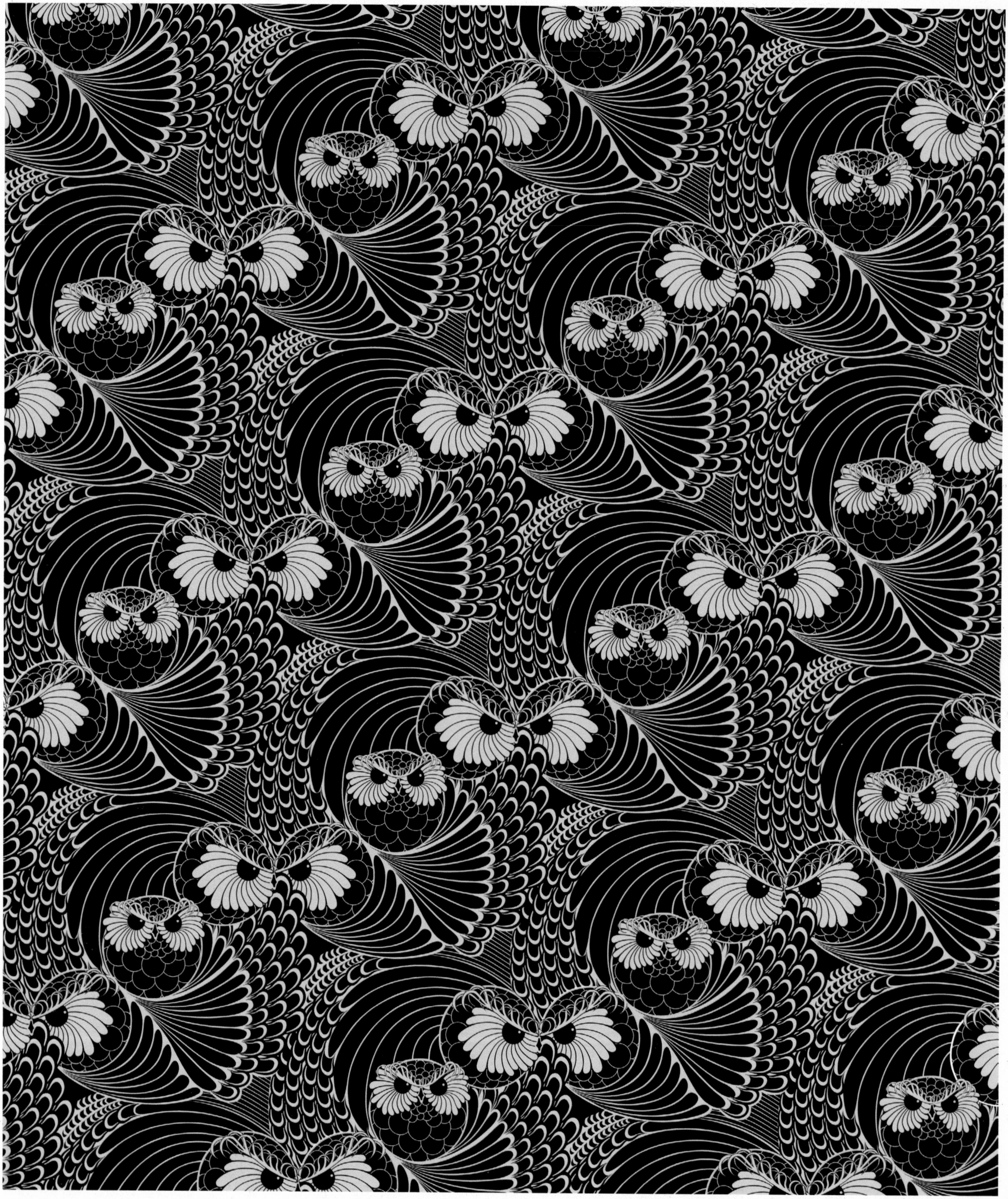

Yehrin Tong Owl - Textile Design, 2005

Yehrin Tong Snake, Tiger, Mermaid – Textile Design, 2005

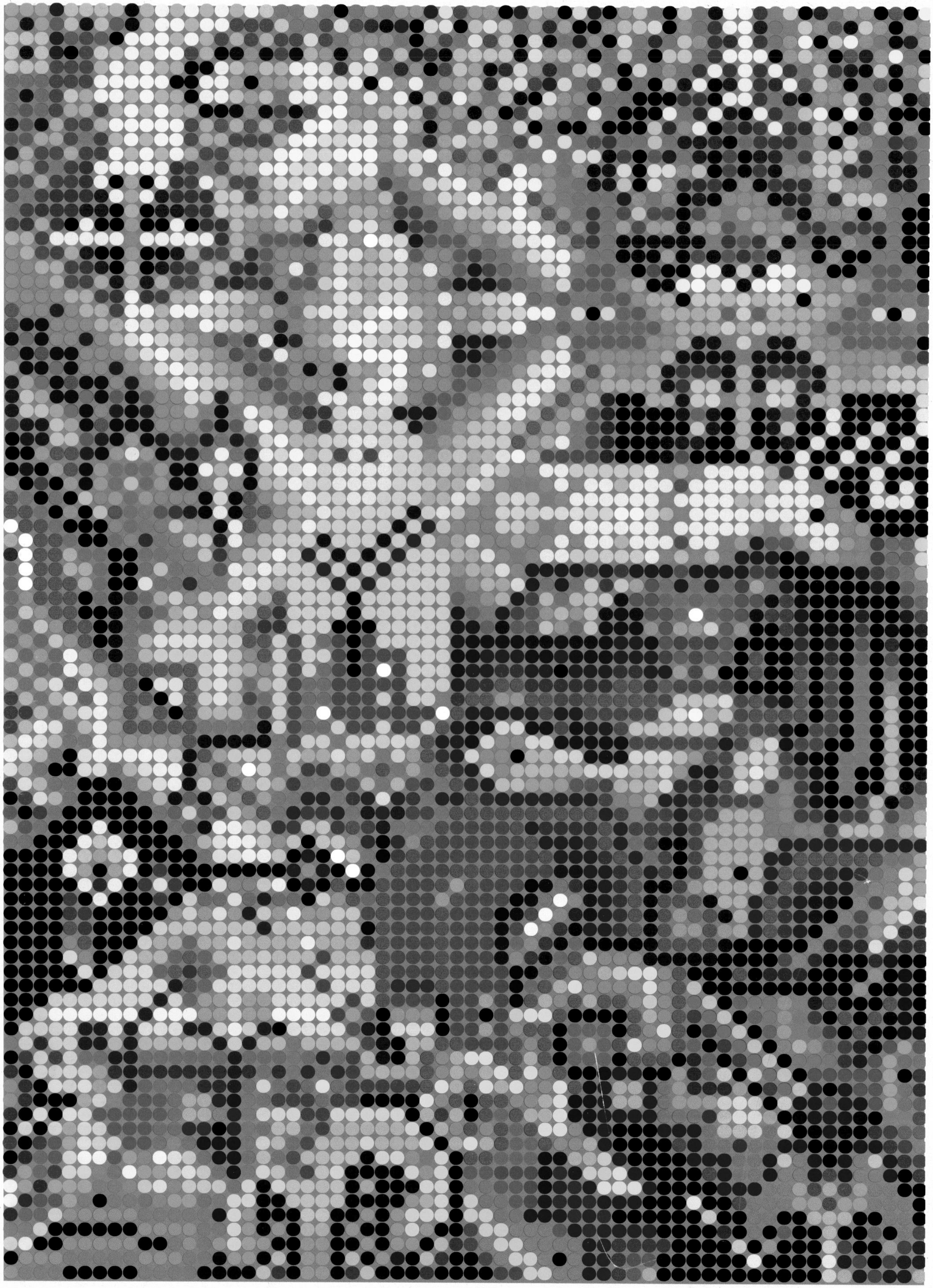

Carlos Otalora Pinta Cielo – Personal, 2008

Carlos Otalora Leichtweber, Madre Selva, Folclor Muisca – Personal, 2008

Kate Sutton Trees - Ad, 2008

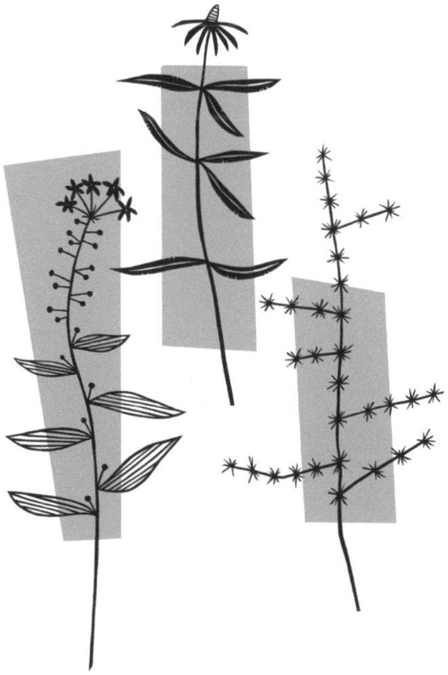

Kate Sutton Birdhouses (left), 2008 **Skinny Laminx** Mountain Garden (middle), 2008 **James Gulliver Hancock** Camera Vision (top), American Bird (right), 2008

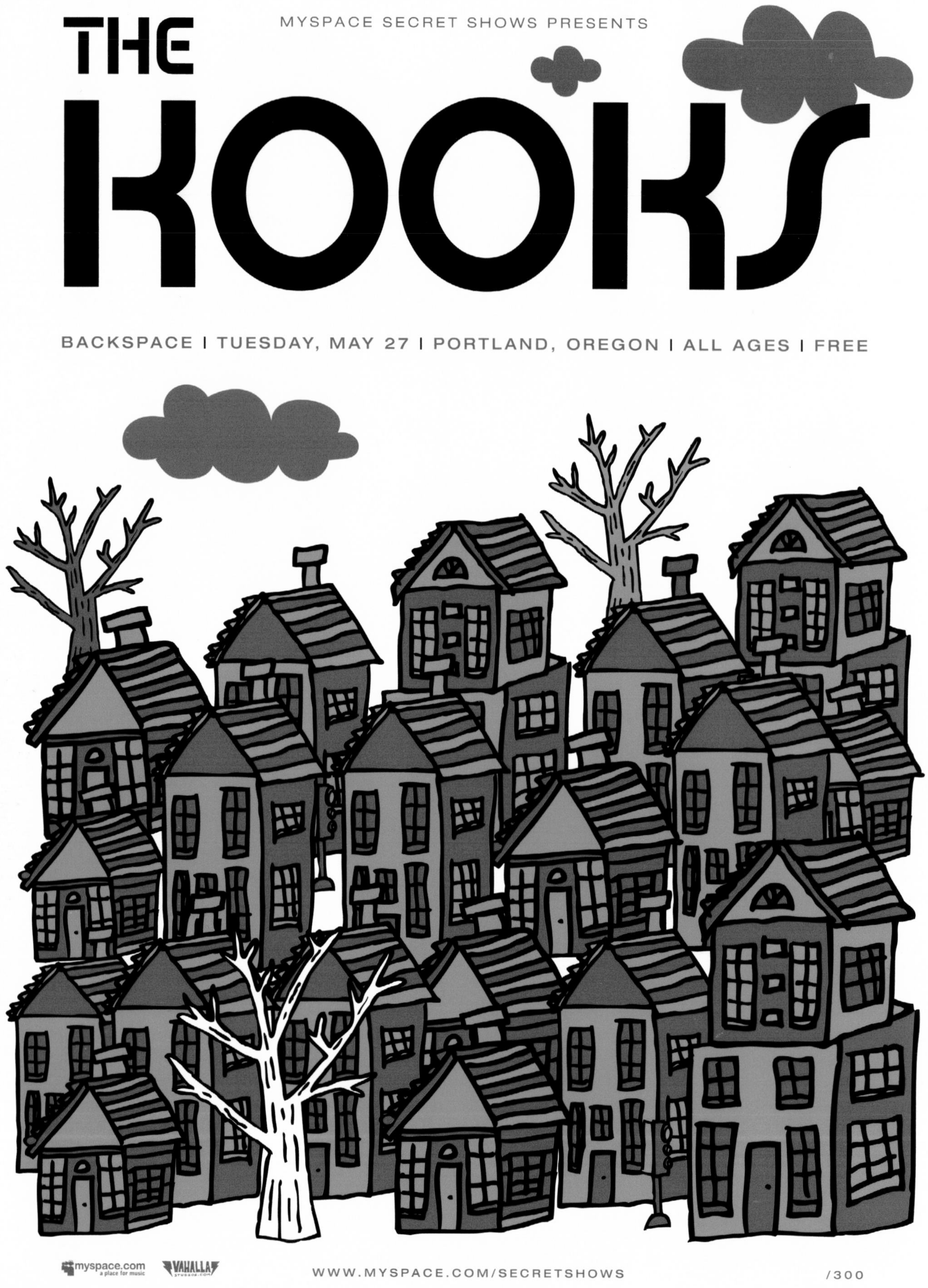

Tad Carpenter The Kooks - Poster, 2008

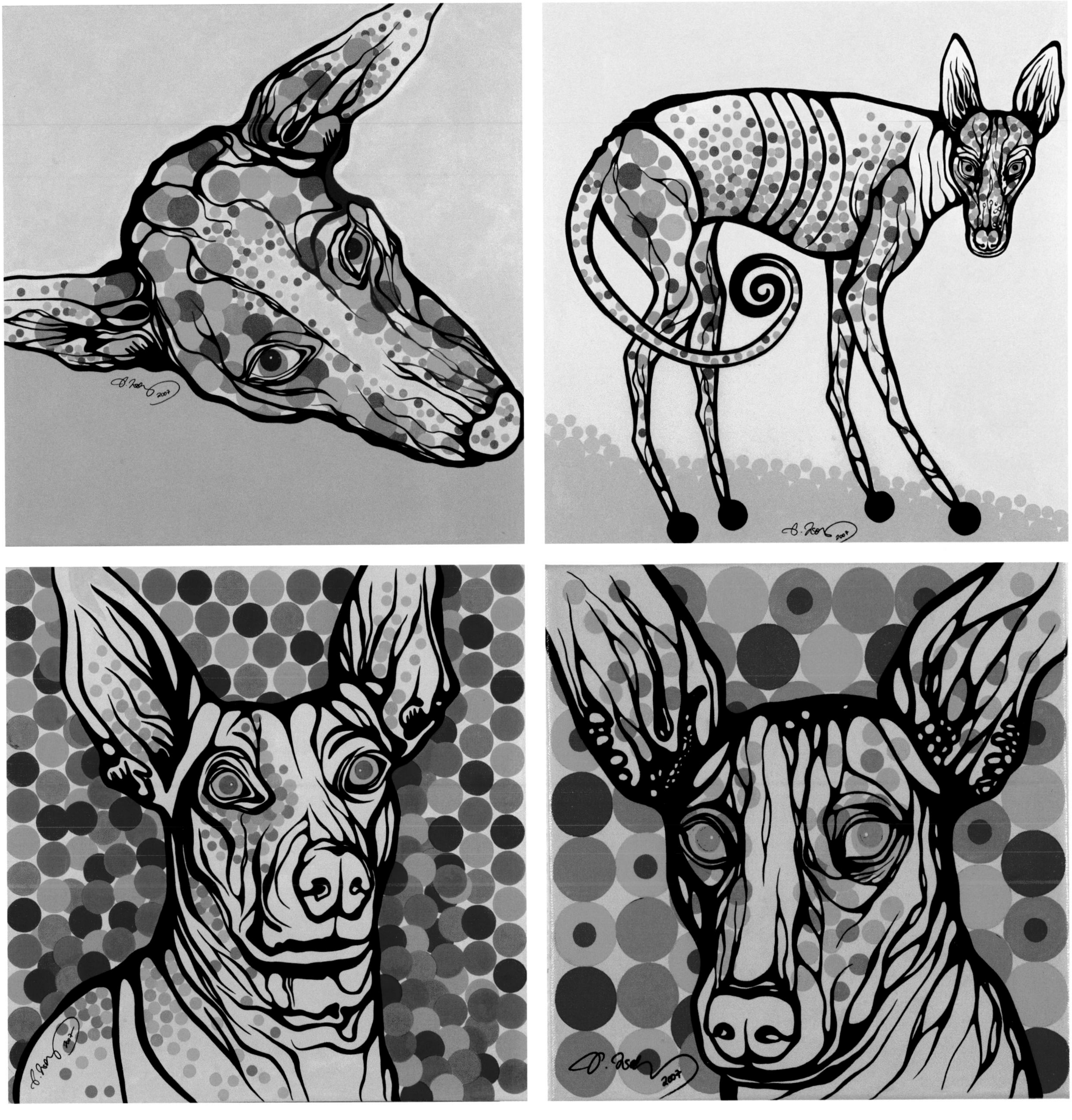

Viola Welker Podencos – Paintings, 2008

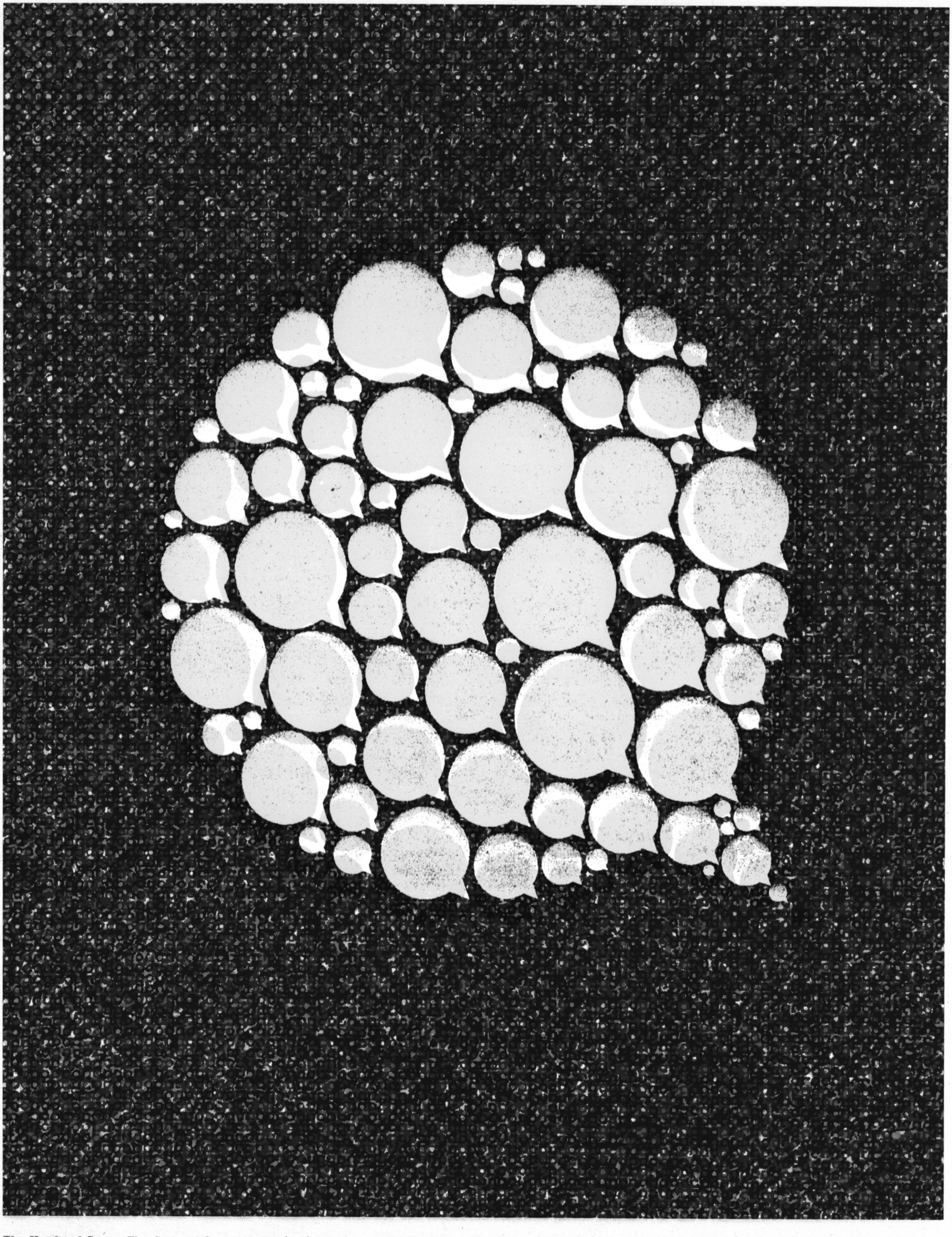

The Heads of State The State of Social Media (left) – Editorial, 2007 **Sellout Industries** Letterism (right) – Textile Design, 2008

IT IS FOOLISH TO
FEAR THAT WHICH
YOU CANNOT AVOID
BE SCARED OF
TYPOGRAPHICALLY
DISORDER
SELLOUT INDUSTRIES
FEAR
KANT

Kate Sutton

/250

Kate Sutton In the Woods - Art Print, 2008

Nate Duval Nighttime in the City - Art Print, 2009

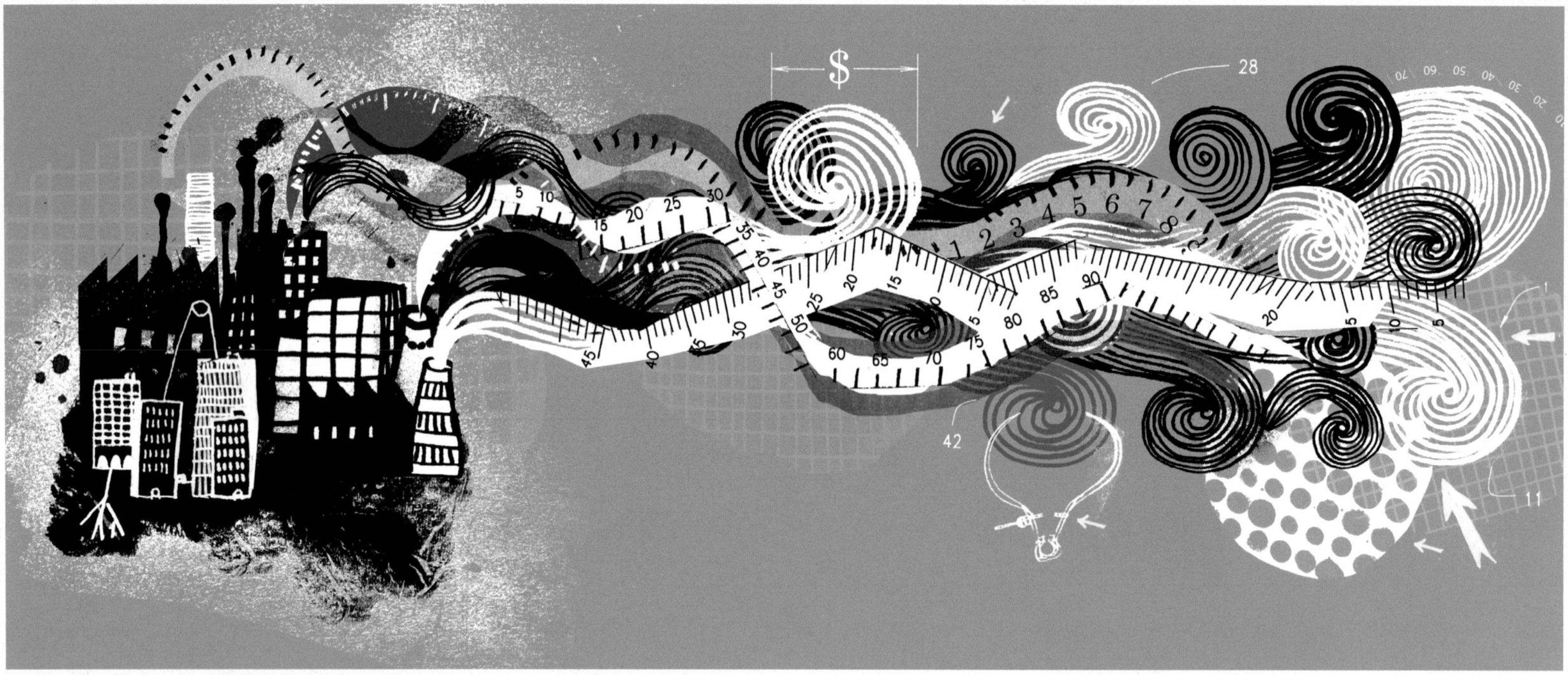

James Gulliver Hancock Cap In Hand (top) - Editorial, 2008 ||| Steinway (left) - Personal, 2008 ||| Josh Pyke (right) - Promo Sticker, 2007

the
NATI NAL
SEPTEMBER/OCTOBER 2007
04 PHILADELPHIA, PA - Fillmore at the TLA *
05 WASHINGTON, DC - 9:30 Club *
06 WASHINGTON, DC - 9:30 Club *
07 CARRBORO, NC - Cat's Cradle w/ Doveman
08 ATLANTA, GA - Variety Playhouse *
10 ORLANDO, FL - The Social *
11 TALLAHASSEE, FL - Club Downunder *
12 BIRMINGHAM, AL - The Bottletree *
14 DALLAS, TX - The Granada Theater **
15 AUSTIN, TX - Emo's w/ Blonde Redhead
16 AUSTIN, TX - Austin City Limits Festival
18 DENVER, CO - The Ogden Theater **
19 OMAHA, NE - The Slowdown **
20 MINNEAPOLIS, MN - The Fine Line **
21 MILWAUKEE, WI - The Pabst Theater **
22 CHICAGO, IL - The Vic Theatre **
23 CINCINNATI, OH - The Madison Theater **
27 SAN DIEGO, CA - The Casbah **
28 LOS ANGELES, CA - The Wiltern **
29 SAN FRANCISCO, CA - The Grand Ballroom **
01 PORTLAND, OR - Crystal Ballroom **
02 SEATTLE, WA - Showbox **
03 VANCOUVER, BC - Commodore Ballroom **
06 BOSTON, MA - Roxy w/ Doveman
07 MONTREAL, Quebec - Le National w/ Doveman
08 TORONTO, Ontario - Phoenix Concert Hall w/ Doveman
11 NEW YORK, NY - Terminal 5
* W/ The Rosebuds + Doveman
** W/ St. Vincent
AMERICANMARY.COM
designed by SPIKE PRESS
printed by DELICIOUS DESIGN LEAGUE

Spikepress The National Fake Empire - Poster, 2008

El Jefe Sharon Jones and The Dap-Kings - Poster, 2008

My Morning Jacket
SEPTEMBER 5th, 2008 • PHILADELPHIA, PA • FESTIVAL PIER AT PENN'S LANDING
SEPTEMBER 5th, 2008 • PHILADELPHIA, PA • FESTIVAL PIER AT PENN'S LANDING
POSTER BY EL JEFE DESIGN • WWW.ELJEFEDESIGN.COM • PRINTING BY GRAND PALACE

El Jefe My Morning Jacket - Poster, 2008

SUNDAY, MAY 13 AT 8PM AT BASS CONCERT HALL
BRIGHT EYES
with Oakley Hall and McCarthy Trenching
AUSTIN, TX

Todd Slater Bright Eyes - Poster, 2007

Tad Carpenter My Morning Jacket – Poster, 2008

JUNE 12, 2007 • THE PALACE THEATER • ALBANY, NY

Todd Slater Ween – Poster, 2007

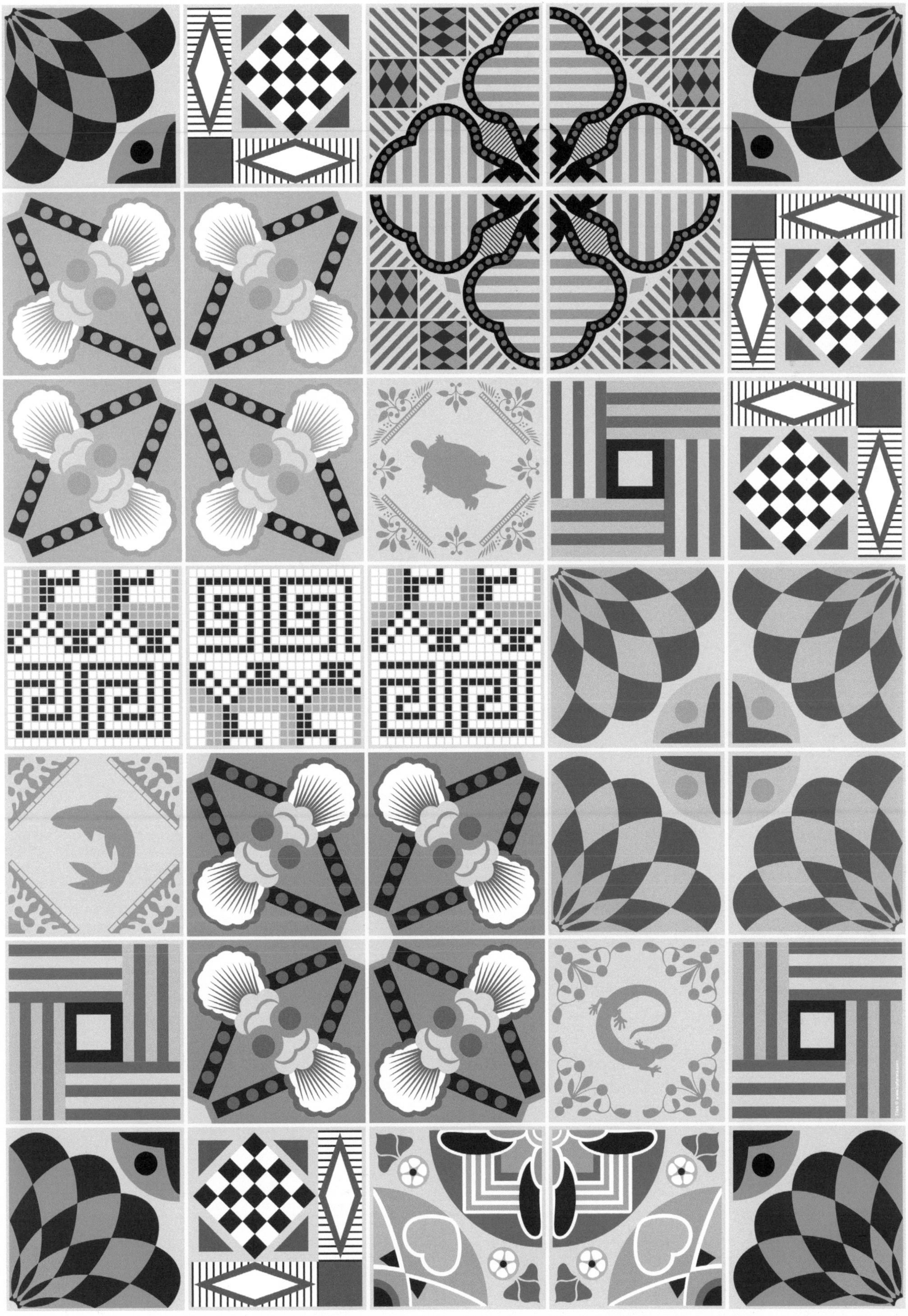

Hanna Werning Tiles – Wallpaper Poster, 2006

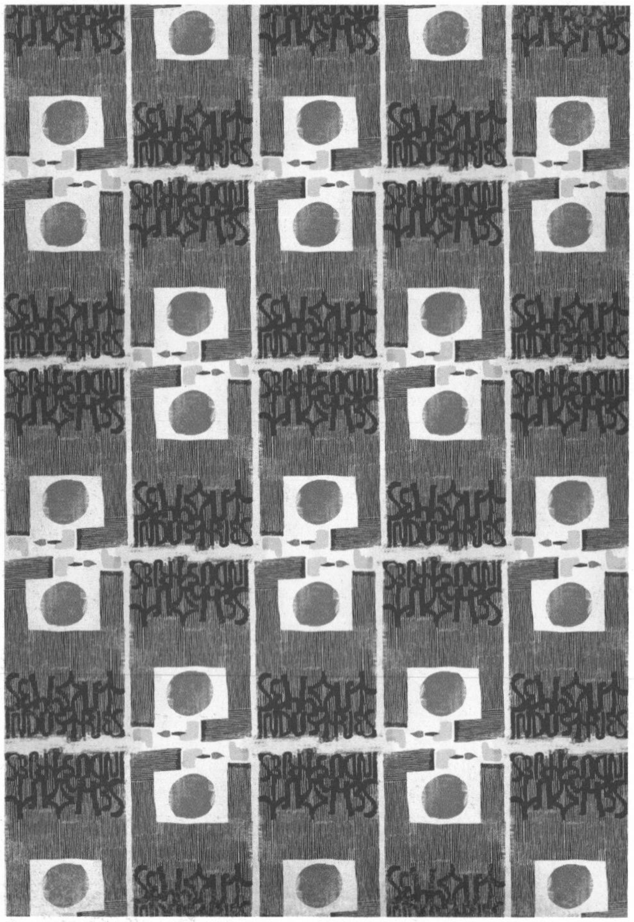

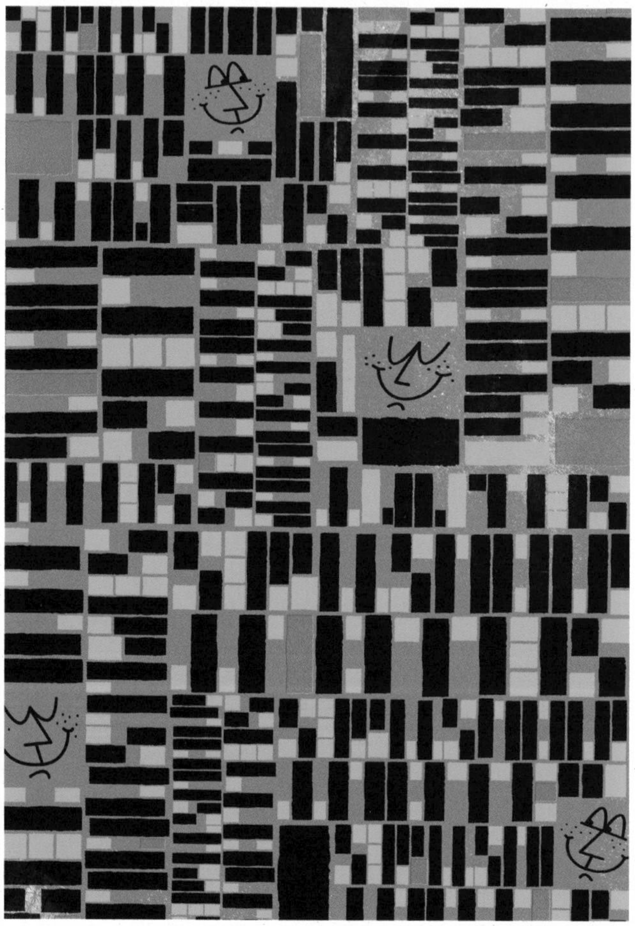

Sellout Industries Painter (top left), Faces (right), Factory (top right) - Textile Design, Editorial 2008/2009 **Helen Dardik** Rainbow Berries (left) - Textile Design, 2007

Sellout Industries Birds (top left), Flowers (top right) – Textile Design, 2008 **Hanna Werning** Cone Shell (left), Hanna W. (right) – Greeting Cards, 2006/2009

Thank you
thank you
THANK YOU
Merci
Thank You
CALL AGAIN
thank you...

General Pattern Thank You – Art Print, 2007

NOW
GO DO
THAT
VOODOO
THAT
YOU DO
SO WELL!
HEDLEY LAMARR 1974

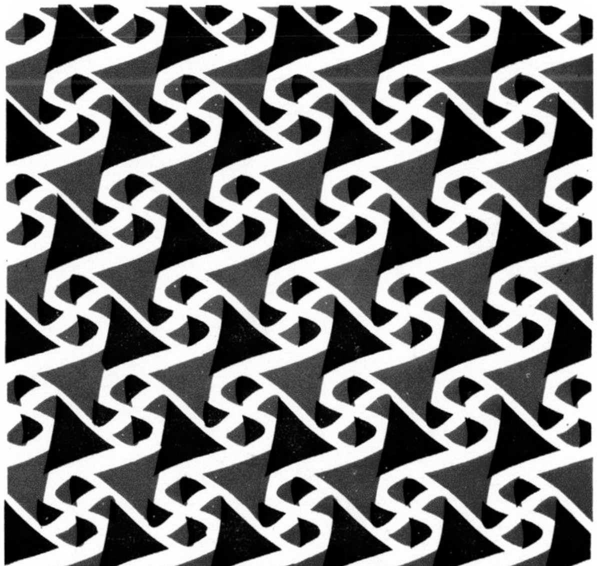

General Pattern Wave (top), Flag (right), Voodoo – Art Prints, 2007/2008

Matt W. Moore BITNB #1 - T-Shirt, 2008

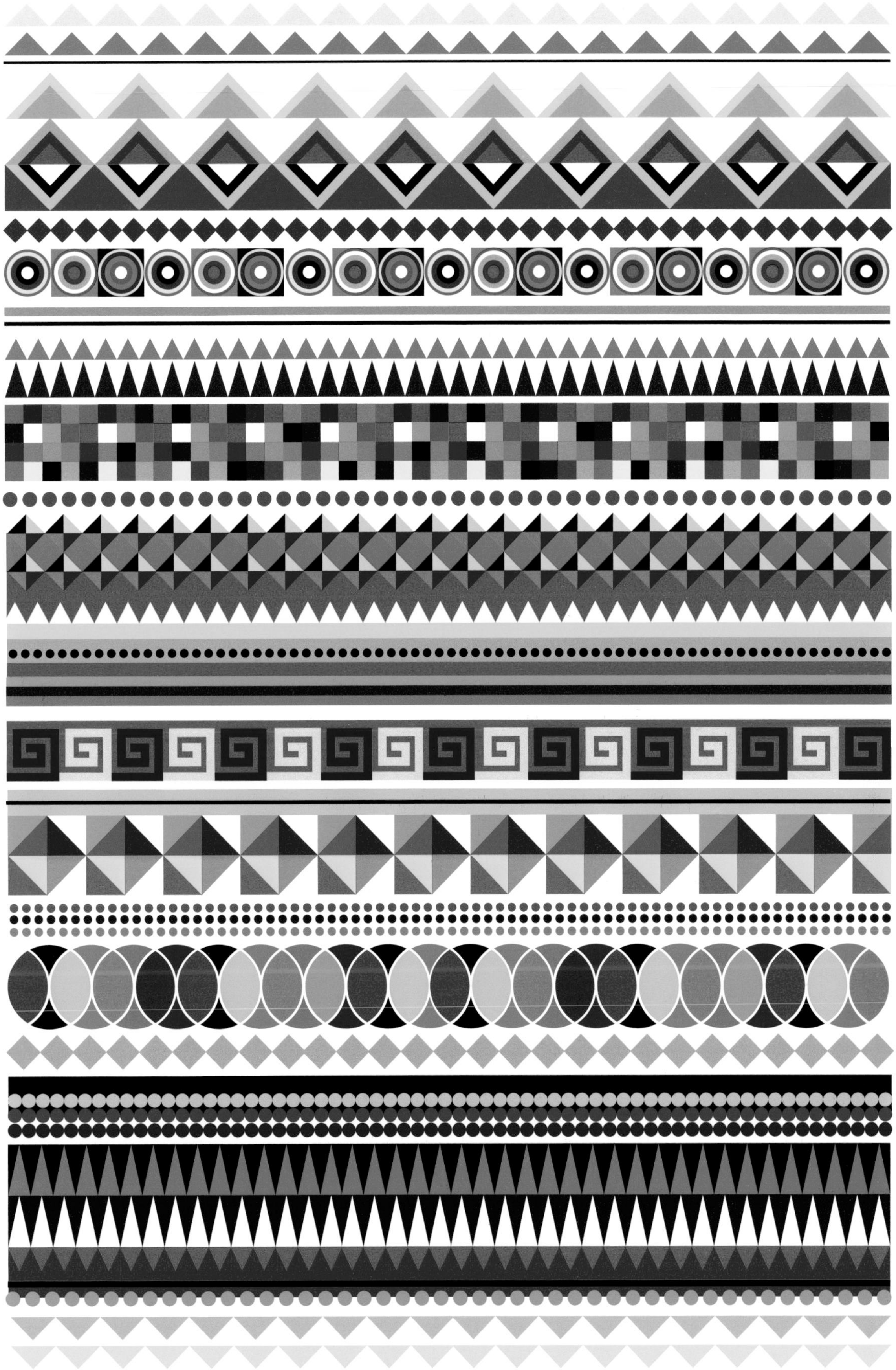

Matt W. Moore BITNB #3 - T-Shirt, 2008

Marcus Walters Abstract (diverse), House – Personal, 2006 / 2008

Marcus Walters Forest-1, Birds-3 - Personal, 2007 / 2008

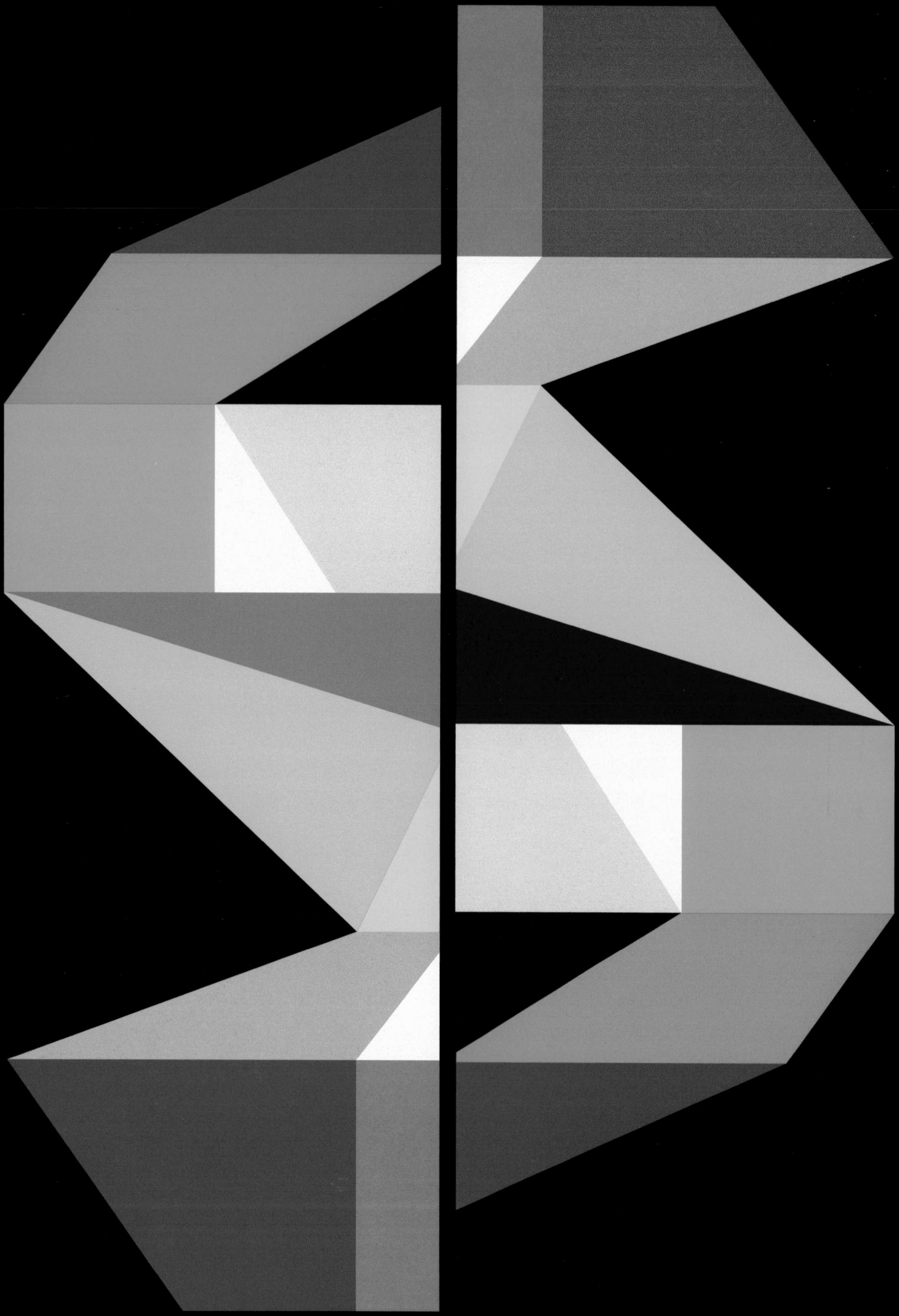

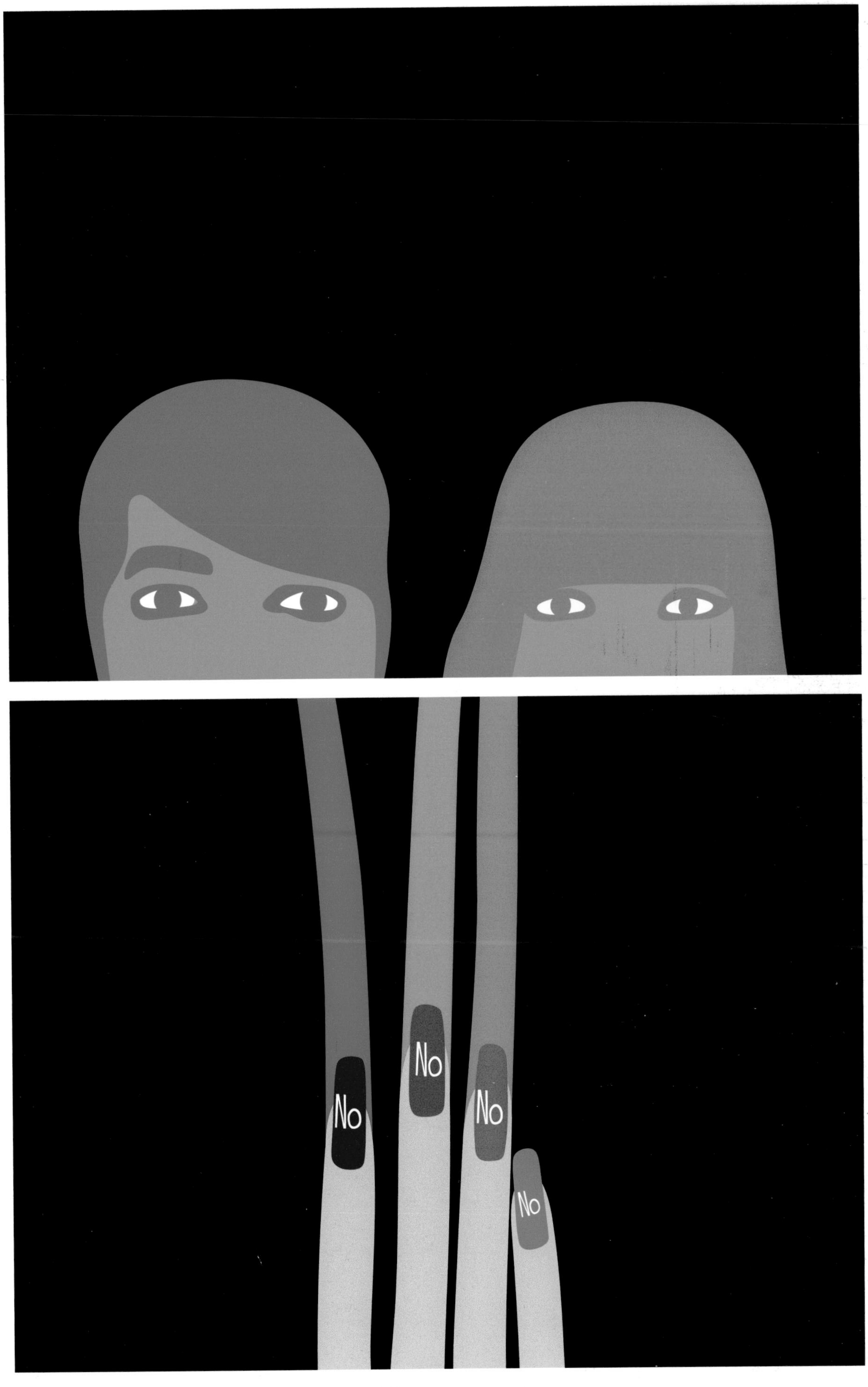

Kari Moden Abstract (left), Boy & Girl, Nails - Ads, 2008

TOM
TYLER
FORWARD
GOING
BACKWARD

A
Drinking Tea From An Empty Cup
Daylight Robbed Her
Moemarer
DC58LP
B
Sialim
Snowball Go Green
DC58LP
The Crippled Diode
In Silico
Give It A Name
C
Backspace Altercation
No Dice
D

La Boca *Forward Going Backward – Album Cover, 2005*

La Boca The Conversation – T-Shirt, 2007

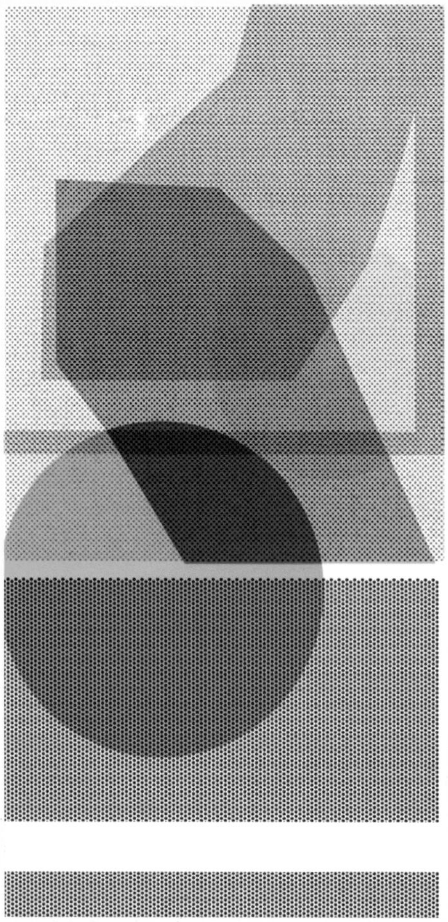

Marcus Walters Summer, Autumn - Personal, 2005 **La Boca** Nightmares On Wax - Record Sleeve, 2008

LOOK
BABY
LOOK

SHINE
BABY
SHINE

RUN
BABY
RUN

Kari Modén Look, Hair, Shine Baby, Run Baby - Personal, 2008

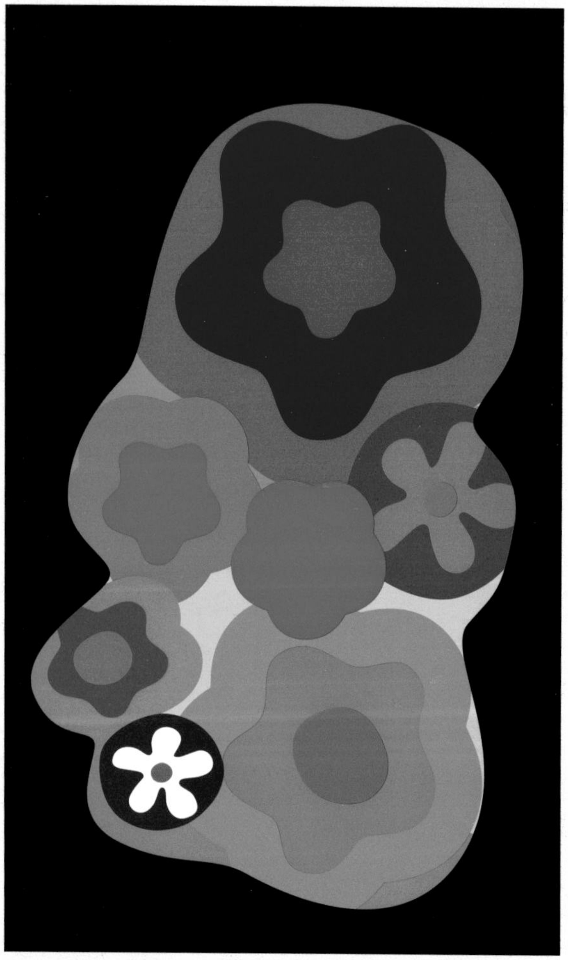

Kari Modén Dating (top) - Editorial, 2007 ||| Flowers (left) - Ad, 2008 ||| Love - Playing Card, 2008

Resistance
is Fertile

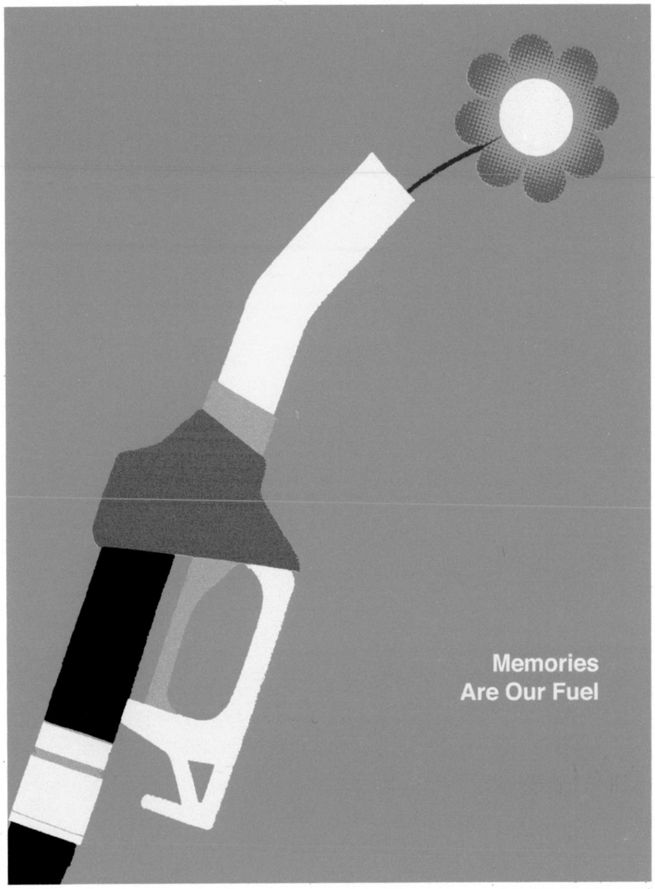
Memories
Are Our Fuel

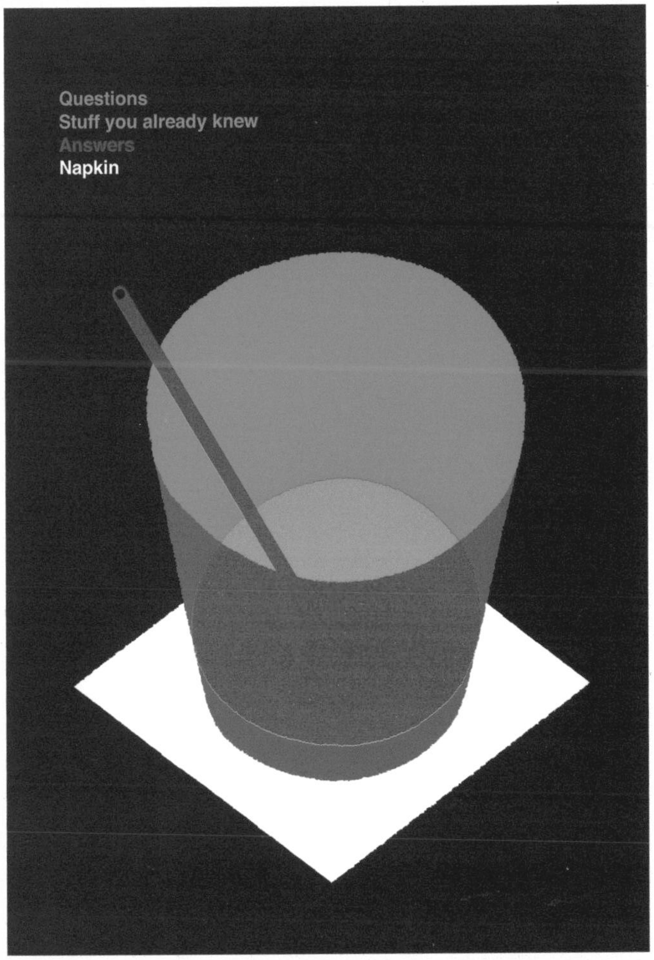
Questions
Stuff you already knew
Answers
Napkin

Make Your Point.

Adrian Johnson Resistance is Fertile, Memories, Answers, Make your point - Posters, 2008

Chris Haughton Digital Digging - Editorial, 2006

Chris Haughton Billybag / Fair Trade Handbag - Textile Design, 2007

Jenny Grigg The Tax Inspector, True History of the Kelly Gang, Illywhacker - Book Covers, 2006.

Jenny Grigg My Life As A Fake – Book Cover, 2006

LONDON
AIRWAVES
FRIDAY 19TH SEPTEMBER 2008
IN SHOREDITCH, LONDON
mr★destiny

Siggi Odds London Airwaves – Poster, 2008

Human Empire Populous, The Year Of, The Horror The Horror – Record Sleeves, 2007/2008

Katharina Leuzinger Kenzo Christmas - Perfume Packaging, 2007

Katharina Leuzinger Kenzo Christmas – Perfume Packaging, 2007

Chickenbilly Flower Beard - Personal, 2008

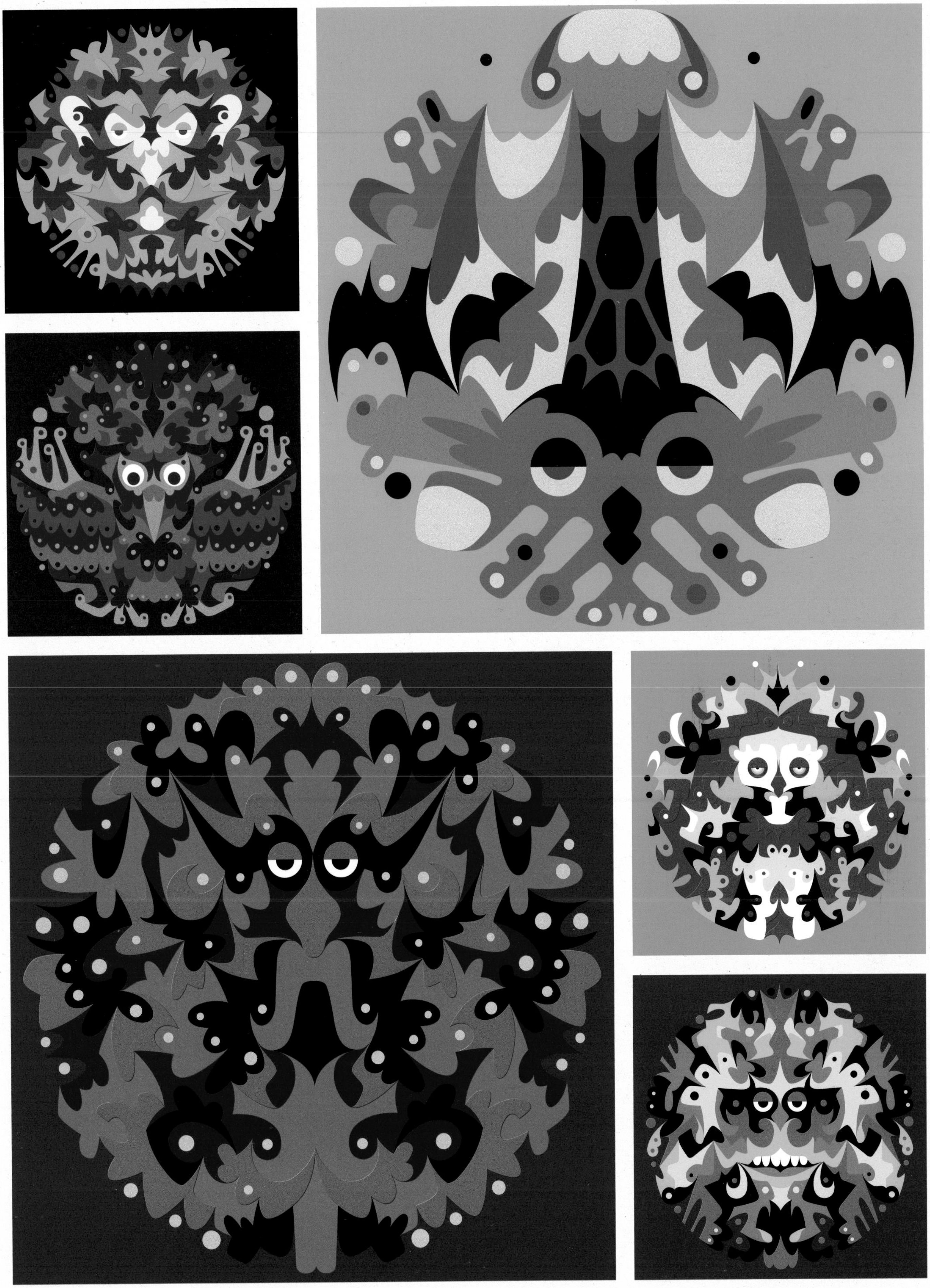

Chickenbilly Deer Hunter, Evening Owl, Sea Bat, Captain Mustache, Cold Turkey, Oz Monkey – Personal, 2008

Peach Beach The Face Tattoo - T-Shirt, 2008

Katharina Leuzinger Untitled, 2008

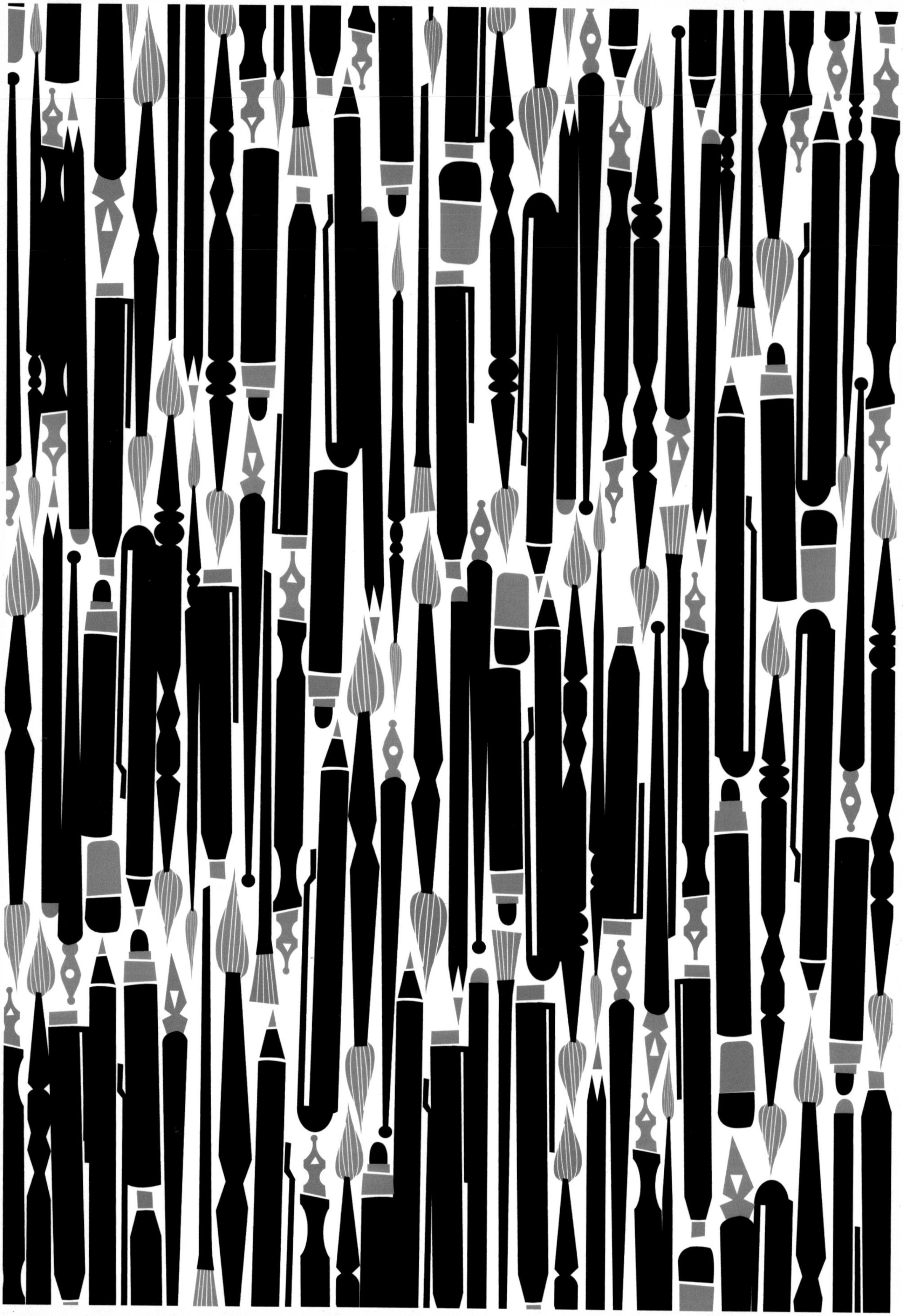

Sellout Industries Stuff Like That - Textile Design, 2009

Skinny Laminx Lava – Textile Design, 2008

Helen Musselwhite Daphne in the Woods (top), 2008
Skinny Laminx Paper Cuts (right) - 2008

TK1
CORNISH LANGUAGE & CULTURAL SHORTS
FYLMOW BERR KERNEWEK HA GONISOGETHEK

A-Side Studio TK1 - DVD Packaging, 2008

Peach Beach Timberland – T-Shirt, 2008

Eva Mastrogiulio The Whale – Children's book, 2008

PB
Intersystems
You don't need vehicles to move something!
www.peachbeach.de
peach beach

Peach Beach You don't need vehicles to move something! – Poster, 2008

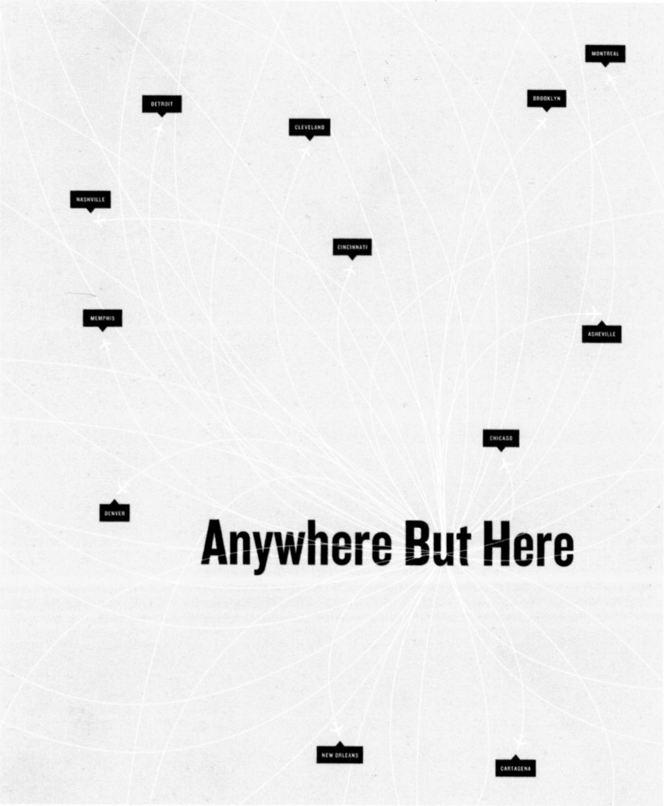

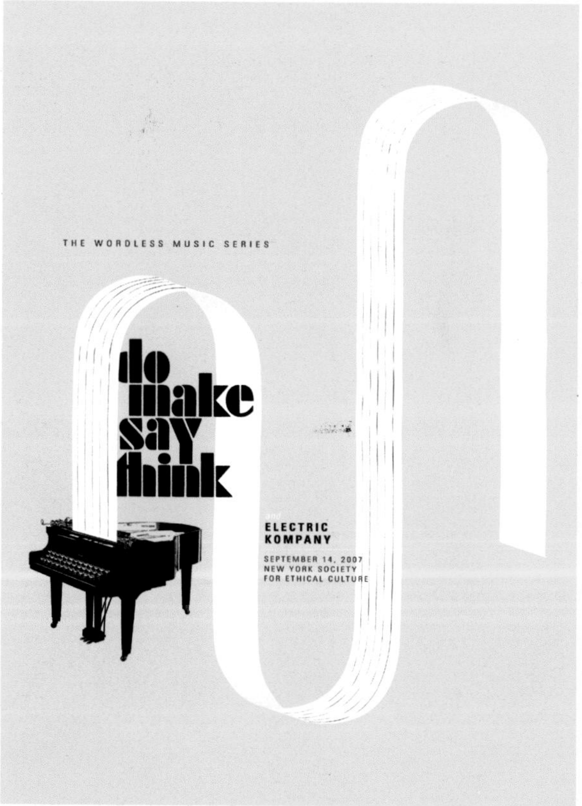

Andrea Guinn International Orientation - T-Shirt, 2008 ||| Anywhere But Here - Editorial, 2008 **Andrio Abero | 33rpm** Wordless Music Series - Poster, 2007

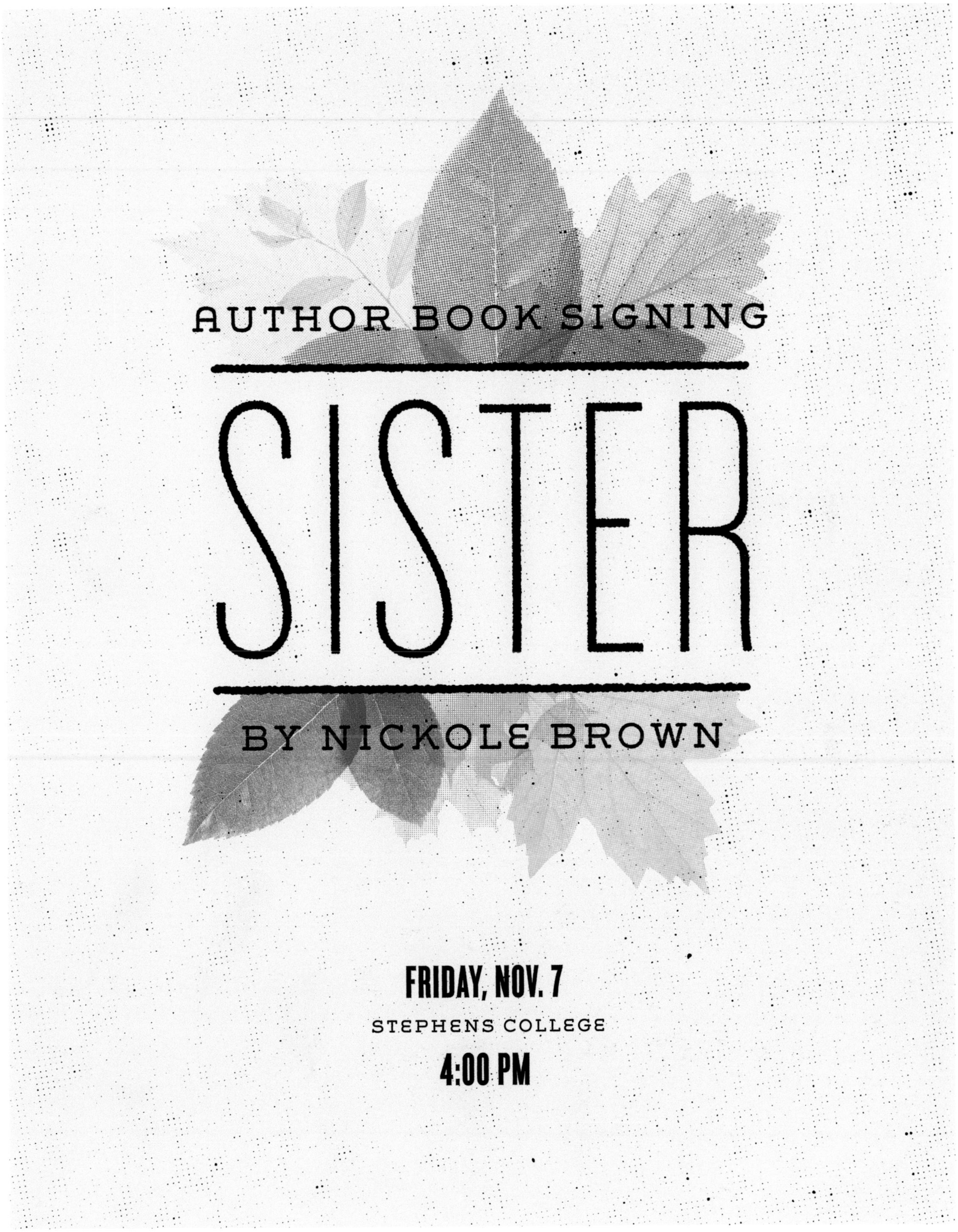

Andrea Guinn Book Signing – Poster, 2008

The Heads of State Obama's New Deal: Let's Innovate - Editorial, 2009 **Silent Giant** Ra Ra Riot - Single & Album Cover, 2008/2009

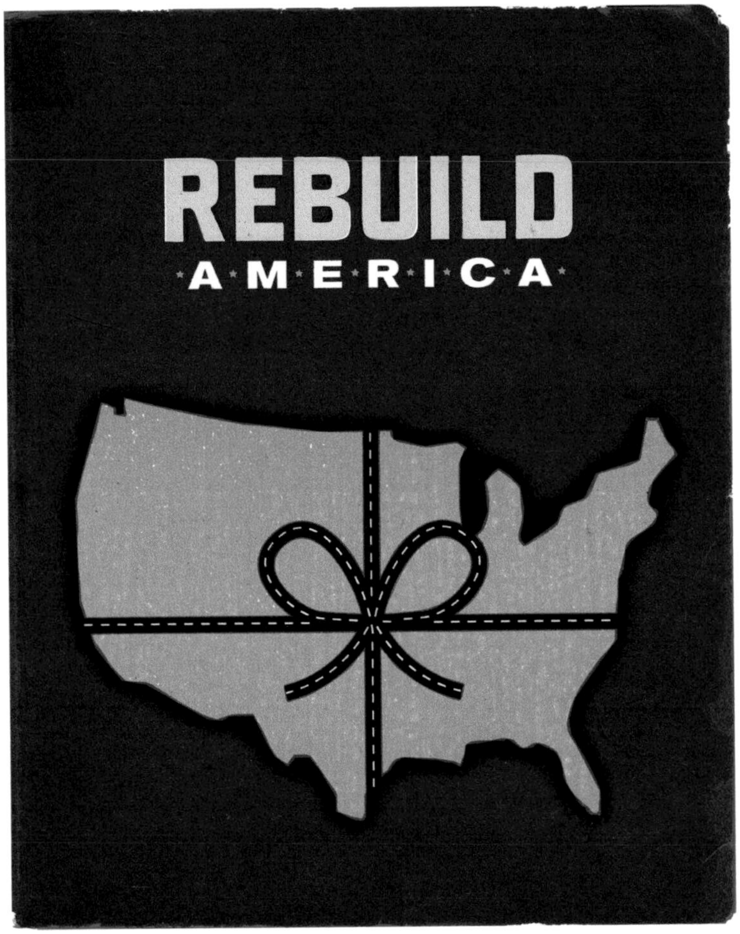

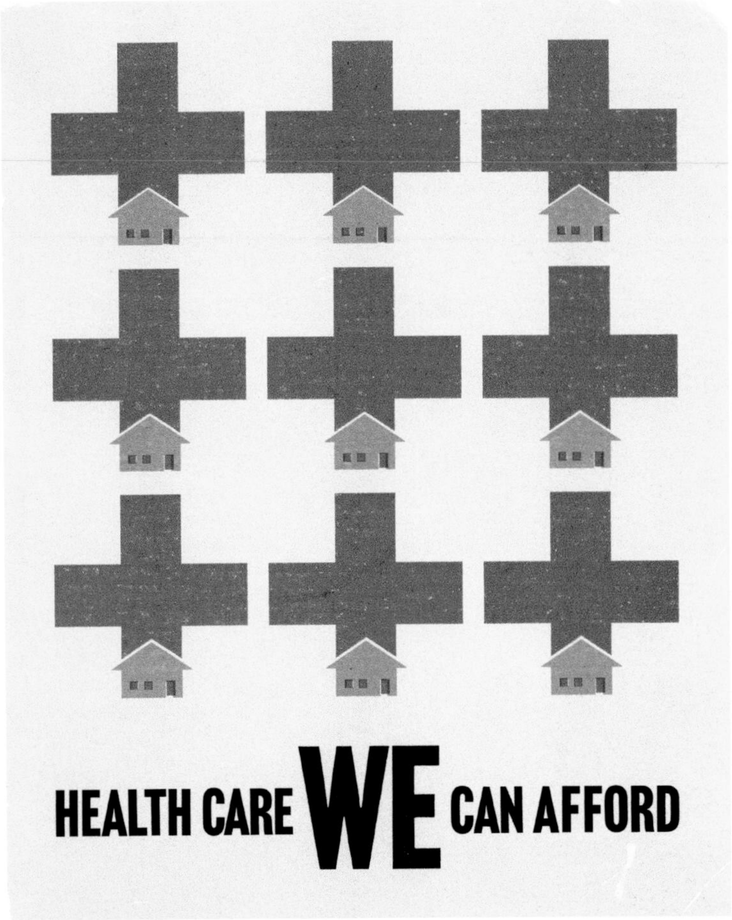

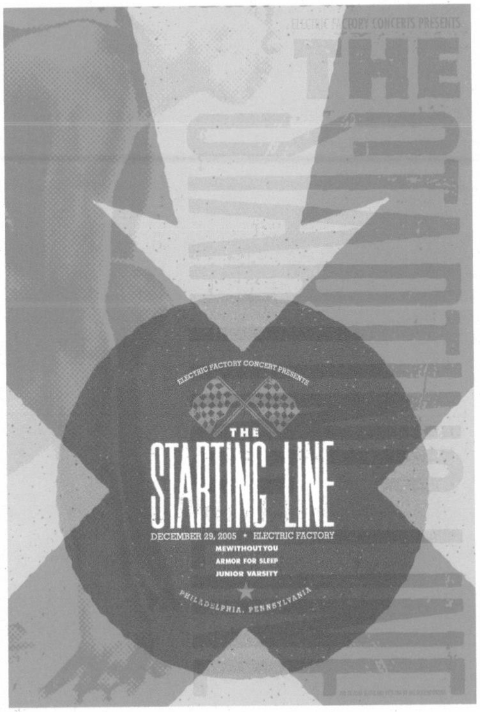

The Heads of State Obama's New Deal: Rebuild America, Health Care We Can Afford - Editorial, 2009 ||| NY Times Magazine - Cover, 2009
Todd Slater The Starting Line - Poster, 2006 **Tes One** Danny - Art Print, 2008

JAY FARRAR
WITH MARK SPENCER
DAY MARS RAY / BRENDON BUTLER THE ECHO LOUNGE
8/6/04

methanestudios.com

Methane Jay Farrar – Poster, 2004

ISLANDS
WITH SOCALLED & SISTER SUVI | SATURDAY, OCTOBER 14 | SATELLITE BALLROOM

Public Domain Islands – Poster, 2006

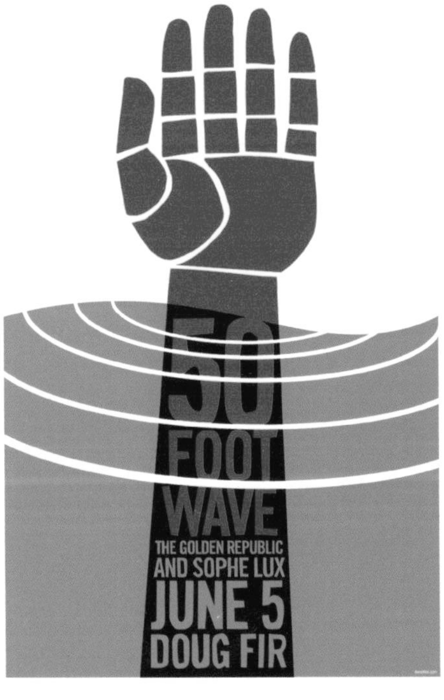

Spikepress Chicago Jazz Fest 2008 - Poster, 2008 **Dan Stiles** 50Foot Wave, Scissor Sisters, Zero 7 - Posters, 2007/2008

Ok Productions
SHARON JONES AND THE DAP KINGS
January 19, 2008 The Variety Playhouse
with THE IVAN MILEV BAND
methanestudios.com

Methane Sharon Jones Legs – Poster, 2008

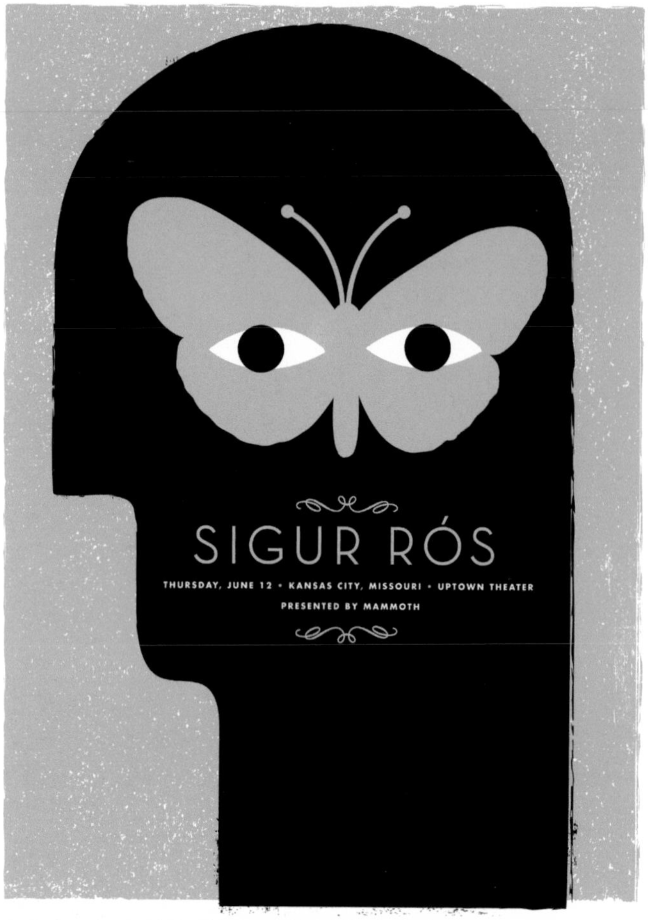

Tad Carpenter Sigur Ros - Poster, 2008 **Hero Design Studio** Decemberists - Poster, 2007 **F2 Design** The Raconteurs - Poster, 2008 **The Heads of State** PIFF - Poster, 2008

The Heads of State Obama's New Deal: Educate for Growth – Editorial, 2009

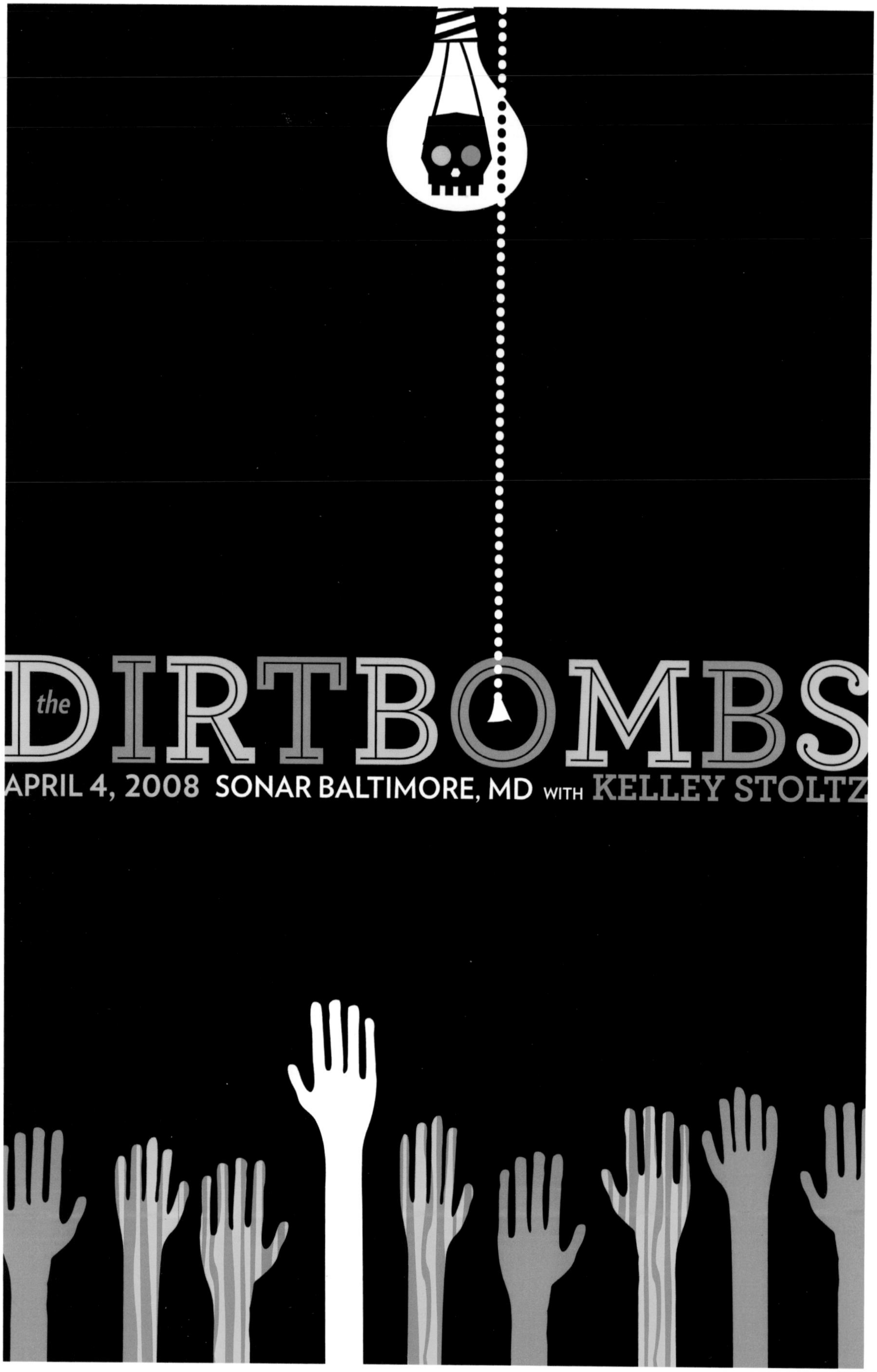
the DIRTBOMBS
APRIL 4, 2008 SONAR BALTIMORE, MD WITH KELLEY STOLTZ

Strawberryluna The Dirtbombs – Poster, 2007

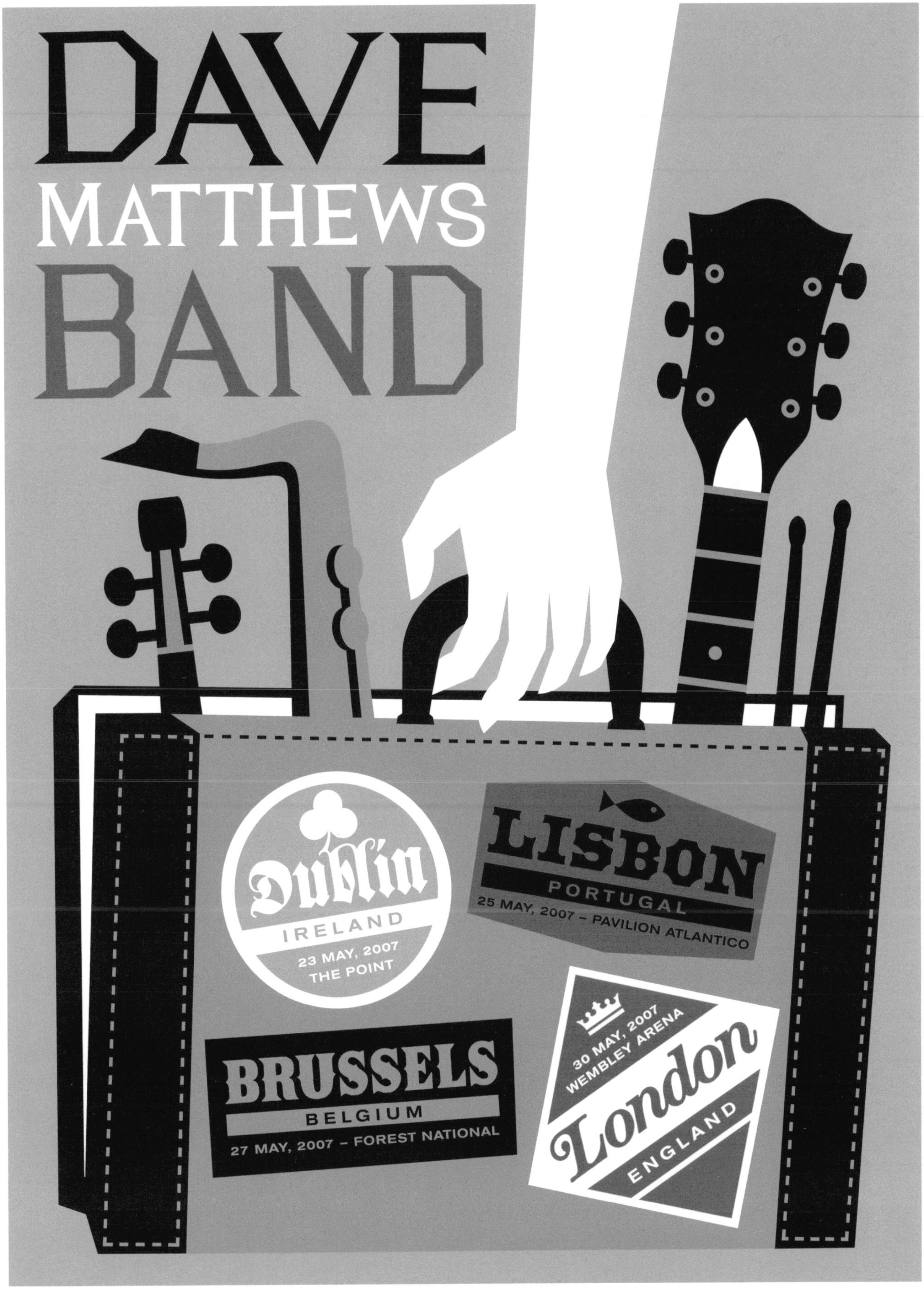
DAVE
MATTHEWS
BAND
Dublin
IRELAND
23 MAY, 2007
THE POINT
LISBON
PORTUGAL
25 MAY, 2007 - PAVILION ATLANTICO
BRUSSELS
BELGIUM
27 MAY, 2007 - FOREST NATIONAL
30 MAY, 2007
WEMBLEY ARENA
London
ENGLAND

Doublenaut Dave Matthews Band - Poster, 2007

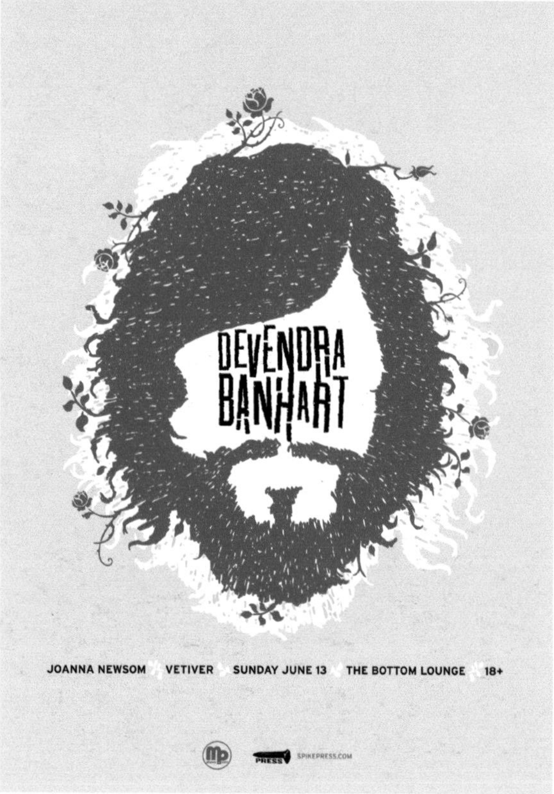

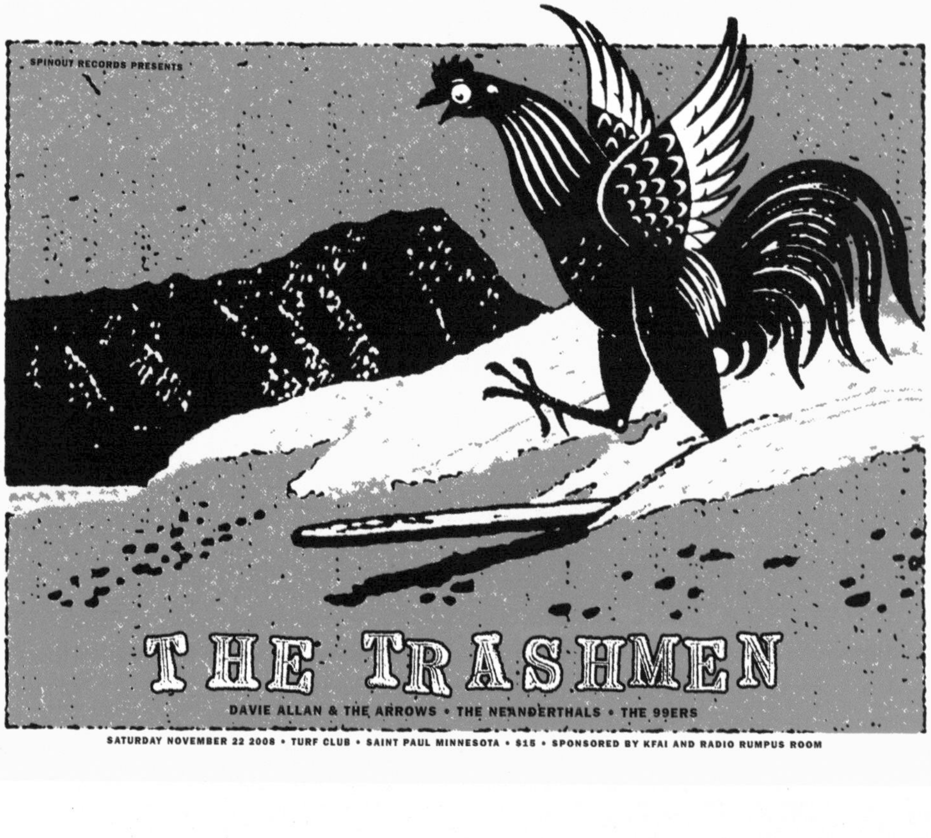

Methane Band of Horses – Posters, 2006/2007 **Spikepress** Devendra Banhart – Poster, 2004 **Amy Jo** The Trashmen – Poster, 2008

Silent Giant Mogwai, Murder Death - Posters, 2008 **El Jefe** Dean and Britta - Poster, 2008 **Methane** Silver Jews - Poster, 2005

EXPLOSIONS IN THE SKY
APRIL 8, 2008
TERMINAL 5
w/ LICHENS

Nate Duval Explosions in the Sky - Poster, 2008

Nate Duval Doodle (top) - Art Print, 2008 **Hanna Werning** Soho Square (left) - Wallpaper, 2008 **Rob Morris** Piece & Love (right) - Poster, 2009

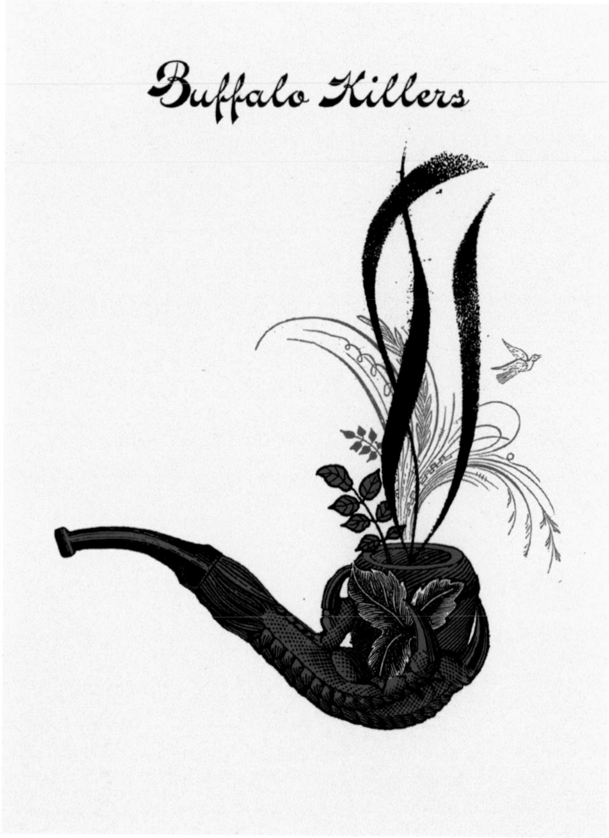

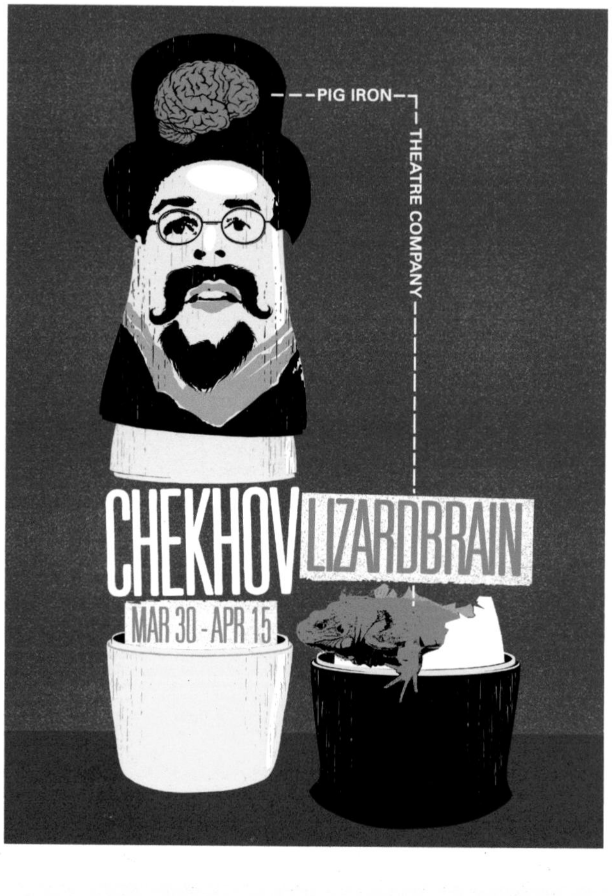

Amy Jo Thrushes / Glasvegas, Buffalo Killers – Posters, 2008 **Doublenaut** Pascale Picard – Poster, 2008 **Andrio Abero | 33rpm** Chekhov / Lizardbrain – Poster, 2007

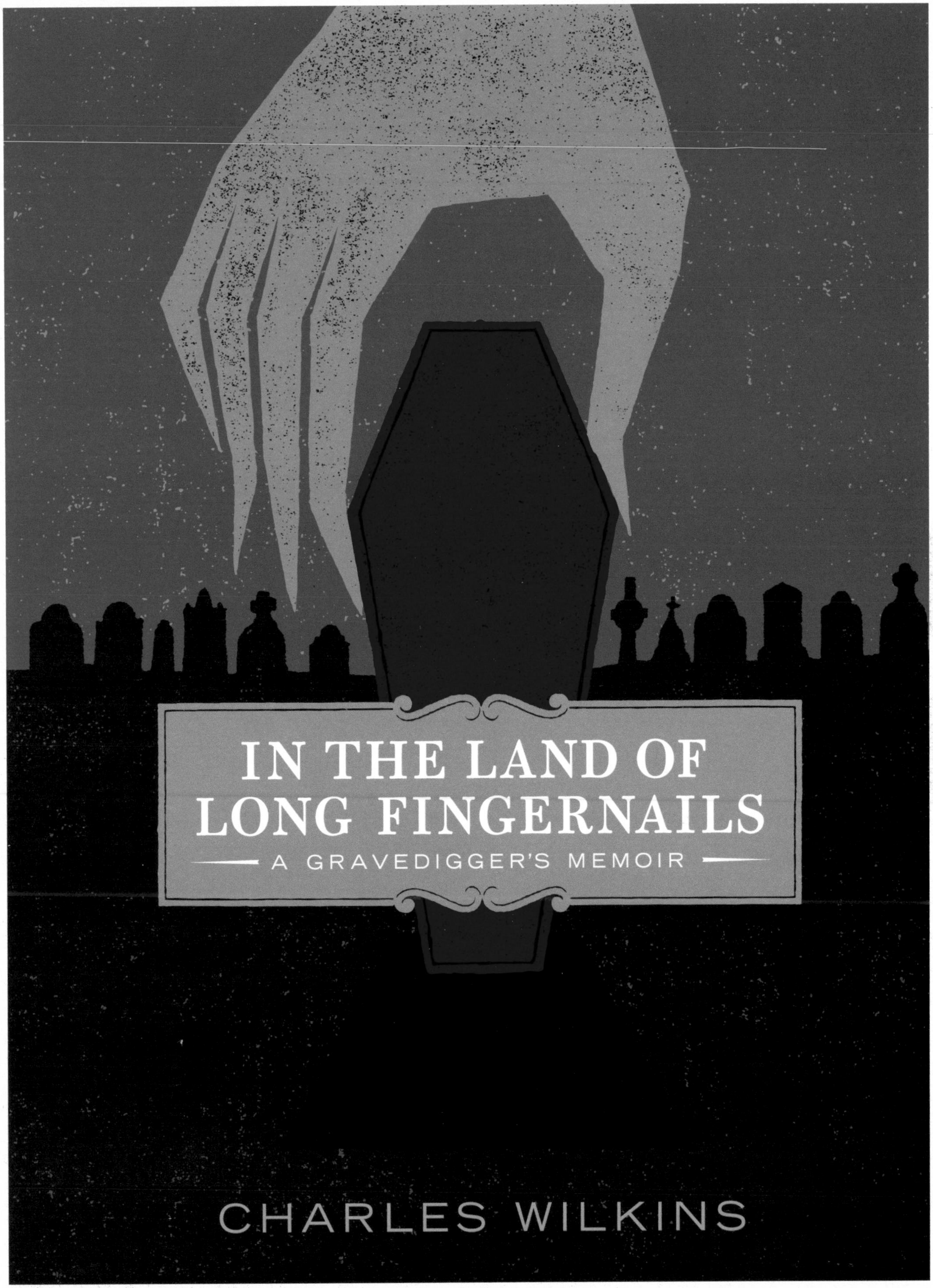

Doublenaut In the Land of Long Fingernails - Book Cover, 2008

BECK
WITH
MGMT
MONDAY SEPTEMBER 29 | KANSAS CITY, MISSOURI | UPTOWN THEATER | 8PM

Tad Carpenter Beck with MGMT - Poster, 2008

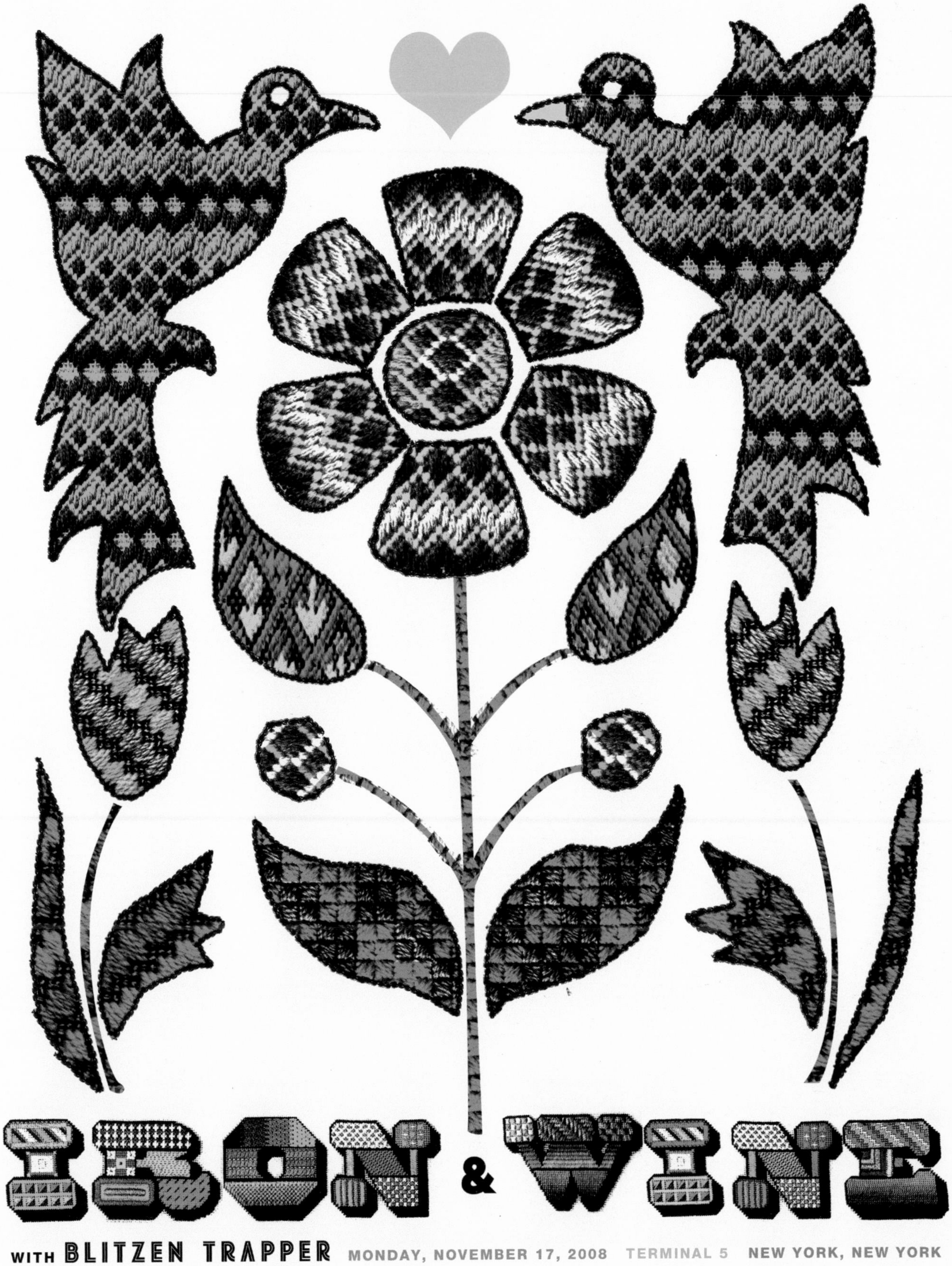

Silent Giant Love Song of the Buzzard – Poster, 2008

Patent Pending Industries Iron & Wine/Calexico, Sleater-Kinney, The Good... – Posters, 2005/2008 **Tad Carpenter** Flatstock 17 – Poster, 2008

Patent Pending Industries Decemberists - Poster, 2007

The Showbox, Monqui, Sealed With A Kiss
and 90.3 KEXP present
February 17th
Paramount Theatre
BRIGHT EYES
JESSE SYKES & THE
SWEET HEREAFTER
with NEVA DINOVA
$21.00 for reserved balcony seating. $23.00 for floor general
admission at Ticketmaster. Doors at 7pm. All Ages
Design by Jeff Kleinsmith. Printed by Patent Pending Press

A Foundation Presentation
July 6 at the Social
IRON & WINE
with
Langtry & Travis Morrison
doors 7PM all ages $10 / $12 day of show tickets PARK AVE CDS, PARK AVE CDS UCF, Ticketmaster

NEKO CASE
with the high dials
april 11, 2006
starr hill

Patent Pending Industries Bright Eyes - Poster, 2004 **Eye Noise** Iron & Wine - Poster, 2006 **Public Domain** Neko Case - Poster, 2006

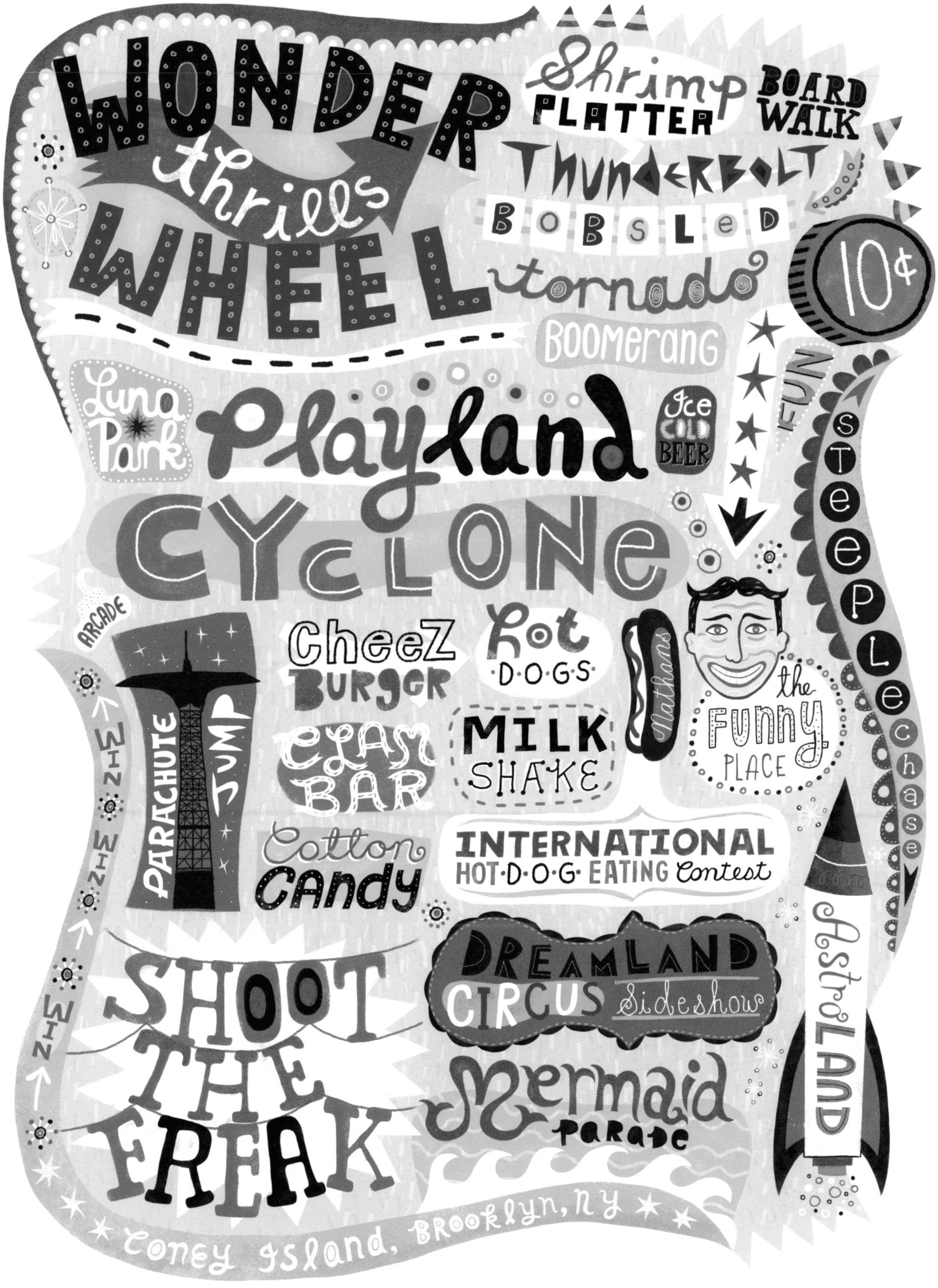
WONDER
thrills
WHEEL
Shrimp
PLATTER
BOARD WALK
THUNDERBOLT
BOBSLED
tornado
10¢
BOOMERANG
FUN
Luna Park
Playland
Ice COLD BEER
STEEPLECHASE
CYCLONE
ARCADE
CheeZ BURGER
Hot DOGS
Nathans
the FUNNY PLACE
PARACHUTE JUMP
CLAM BAR
MILK SHAKE
WIN WIN WIN WIN
Cotton CANDY
INTERNATIONAL
HOT·D·O·G· EATING Contest
AstroLAND
DREAMLAND
CIRCUS Sideshow
SHOOT THE FREAK
Mermaid PARADE
Coney Island, BROOKLYN, NY

Linzie Hunter Coney - Personal, 2008

Doublenaut Passenger Action - Poster, 2008

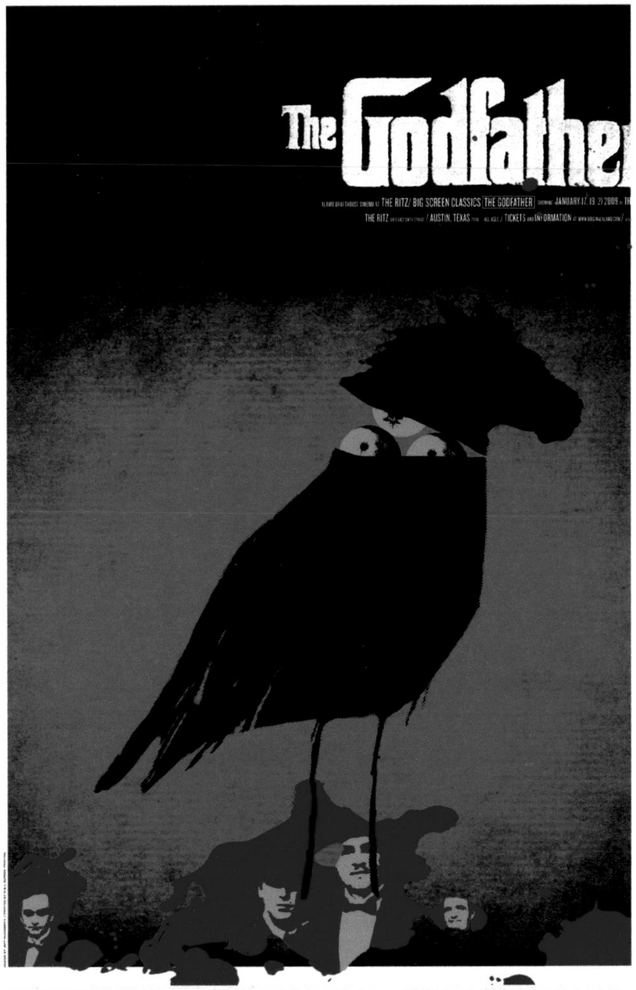

Patent Pending Industries Godfather – Poster, 2009 **Doublenaut** Dave Matthews Band – Poster, 2007 **F2 Design** Ramblin' Jack Elliott, Scott H. Biram – Posters, 2005

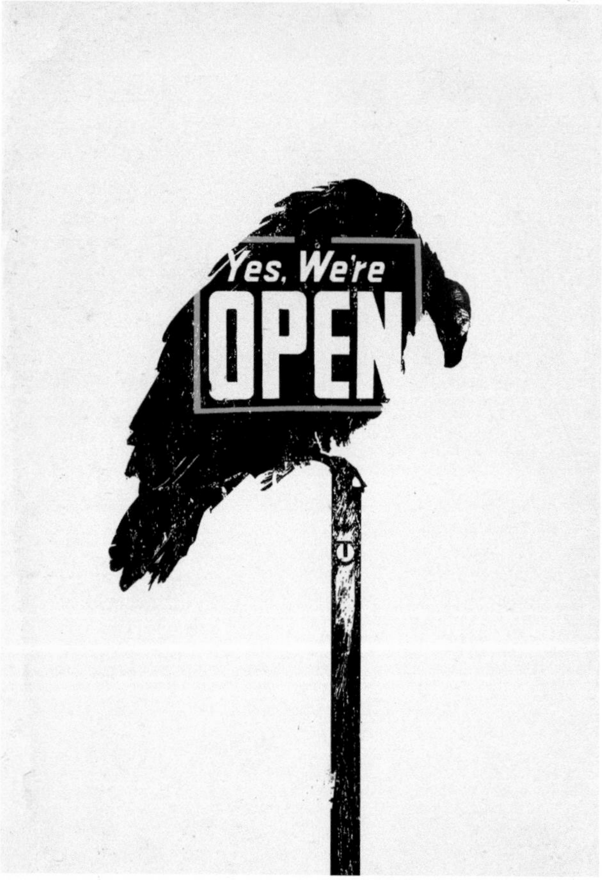

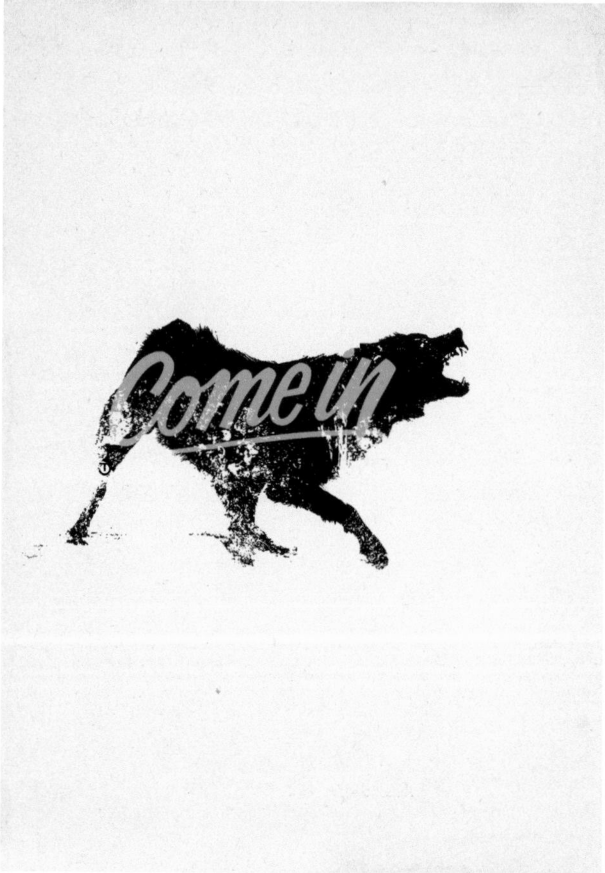

Silent Giant Bon Iver – Art Print, 2008 **Tes One** Open Season, Dog Friendly – Art Prints, 2009

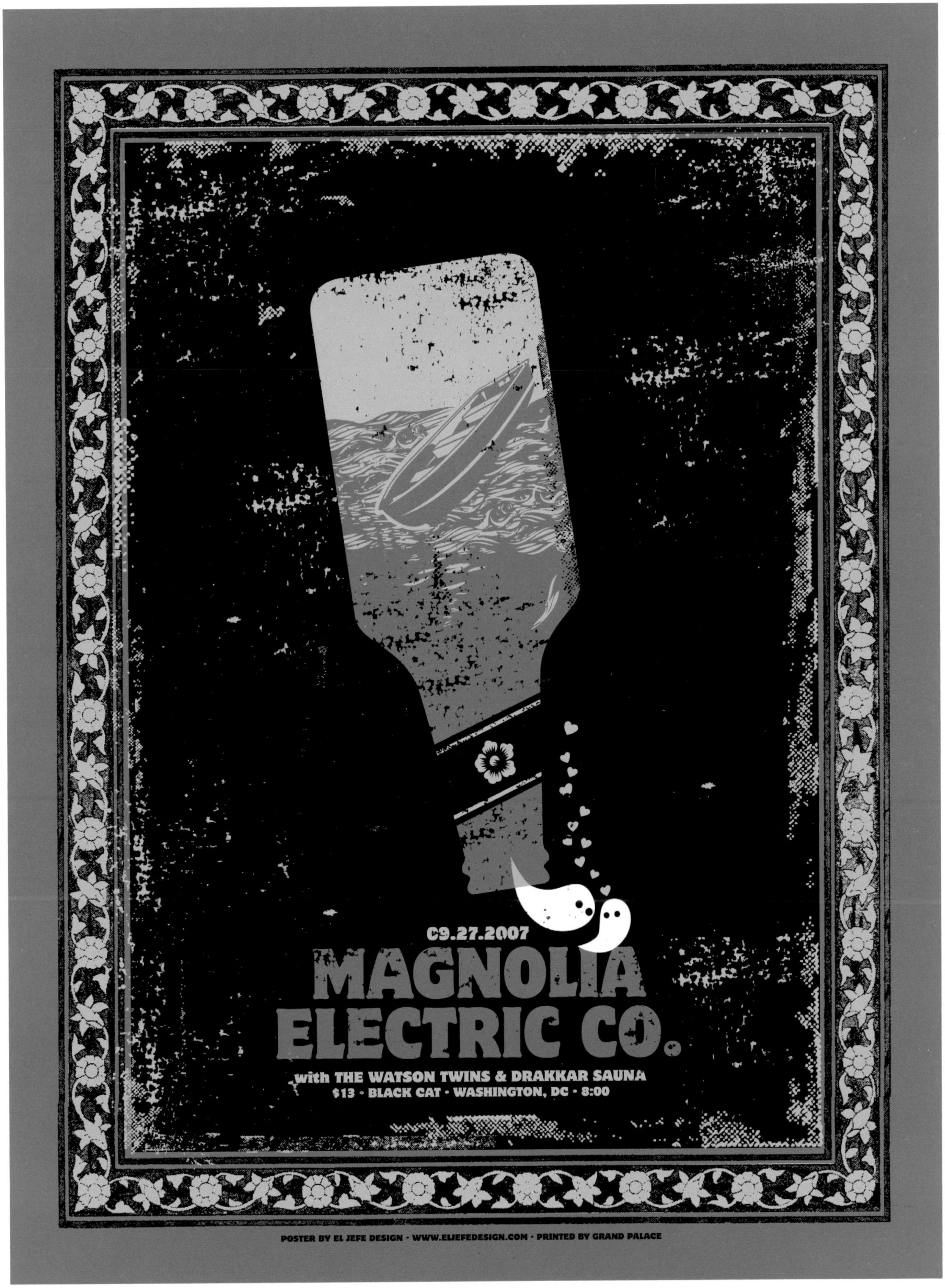
09.27.2007
MAGNOLIA
ELECTRIC CO.
with THE WATSON TWINS & DRAKKAR SAUNA
$13 · BLACK CAT · WASHINGTON, DC · 8:00
POSTER BY EL JEFE DESIGN · WWW.ELJEFEDESIGN.COM · PRINTED BY GRAND PALACE

El Jefe Magnolia Electric Company – Poster, 2007

GOOD
CHARLOTTE
23 MARCH, 2005 | ROCK CITY | WITH MILLENCOLIN
AGES 14 AND UP AND THE DOORS OPEN AT 7:30 PM
ART: TODD SLATER PRINTING: D&L SCREENPRINTING RGG 62 WWW.RICHARDGOODALLGALLERY.COM

Todd Slater Good Charlotte – Poster, 2006

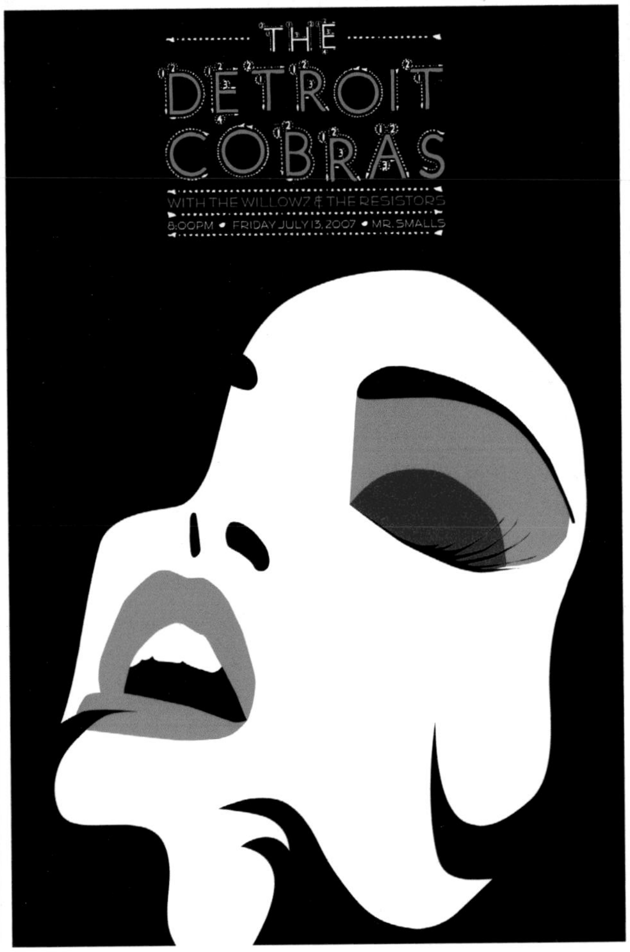

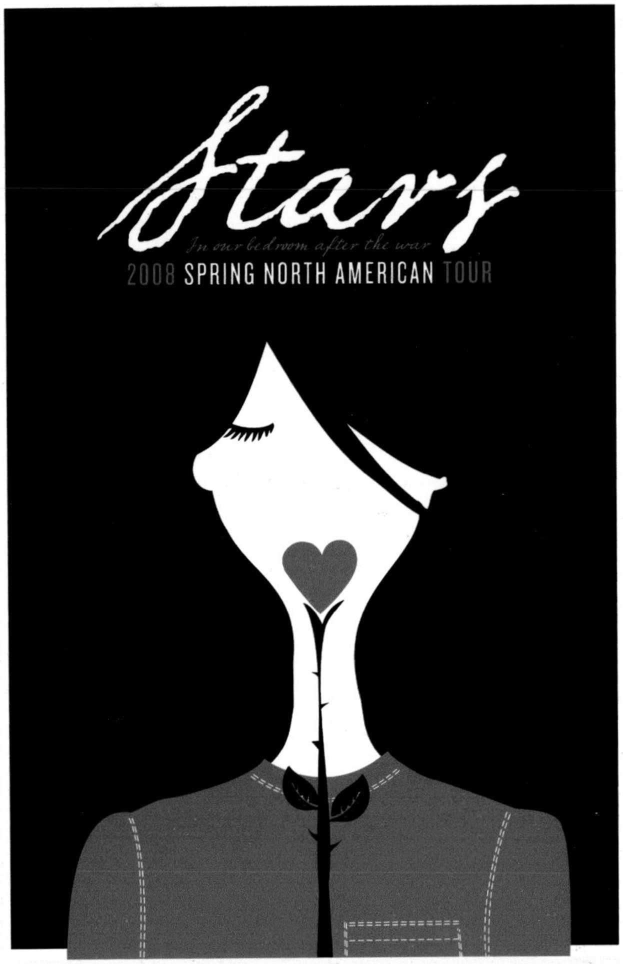

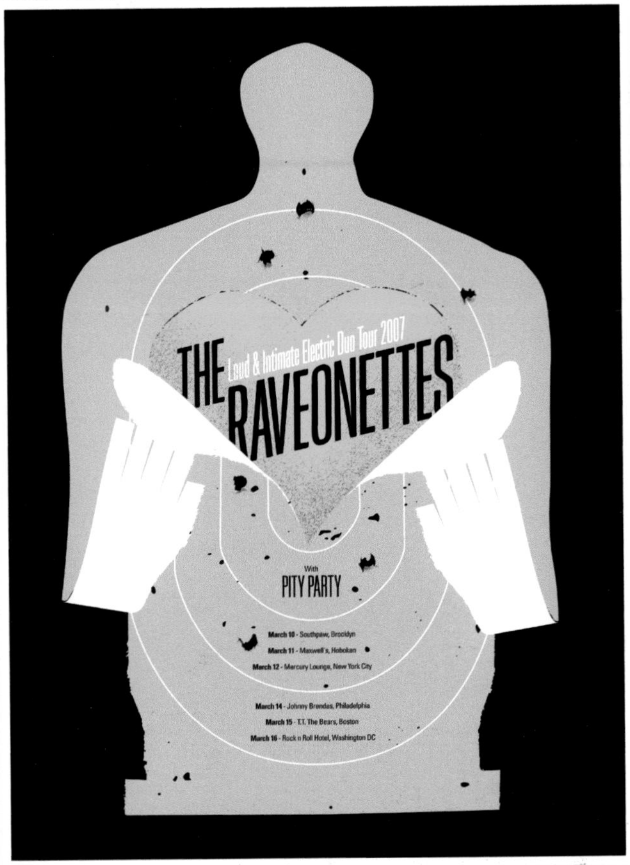

Strawberryluna The Detroit Cobras, Stars – Posters, 2007/2008 **Andrio Abero | 33rpm** The Raveonettes – Poster, 2007 **Eye Noise** The Hold Steady – Poster, 2007

the
Detroit
Cobras
DAN SARTAIN WILLOWZ HOLY PYTHON
DOORS 8 PM • TICKETS $12 21+ • $14 UNDER 21 • THIS SHOW IS 18+
CREEPY CRAWL AUGUST 27
A MIKE JUDY PRESENTATION • AN EYE NOISE POSTER www.eyenoise.net

Eye Noise The Detroit Cobras – Poster, 2007

AEG LIVE PRESENTS
DEATH CAB FOR CUTIE
WITH ROGUE WAVE · MAY 28 2008 · RED ROCKS · DENVER, CO

Dan Stiles Death Cab for Cutie – Poster, 2008

Dungen
WITH NETHERS • WEDNESDAY, JUNE 14 • BLACK CAT • $13

Public Domain Dungen - Poster, 2007

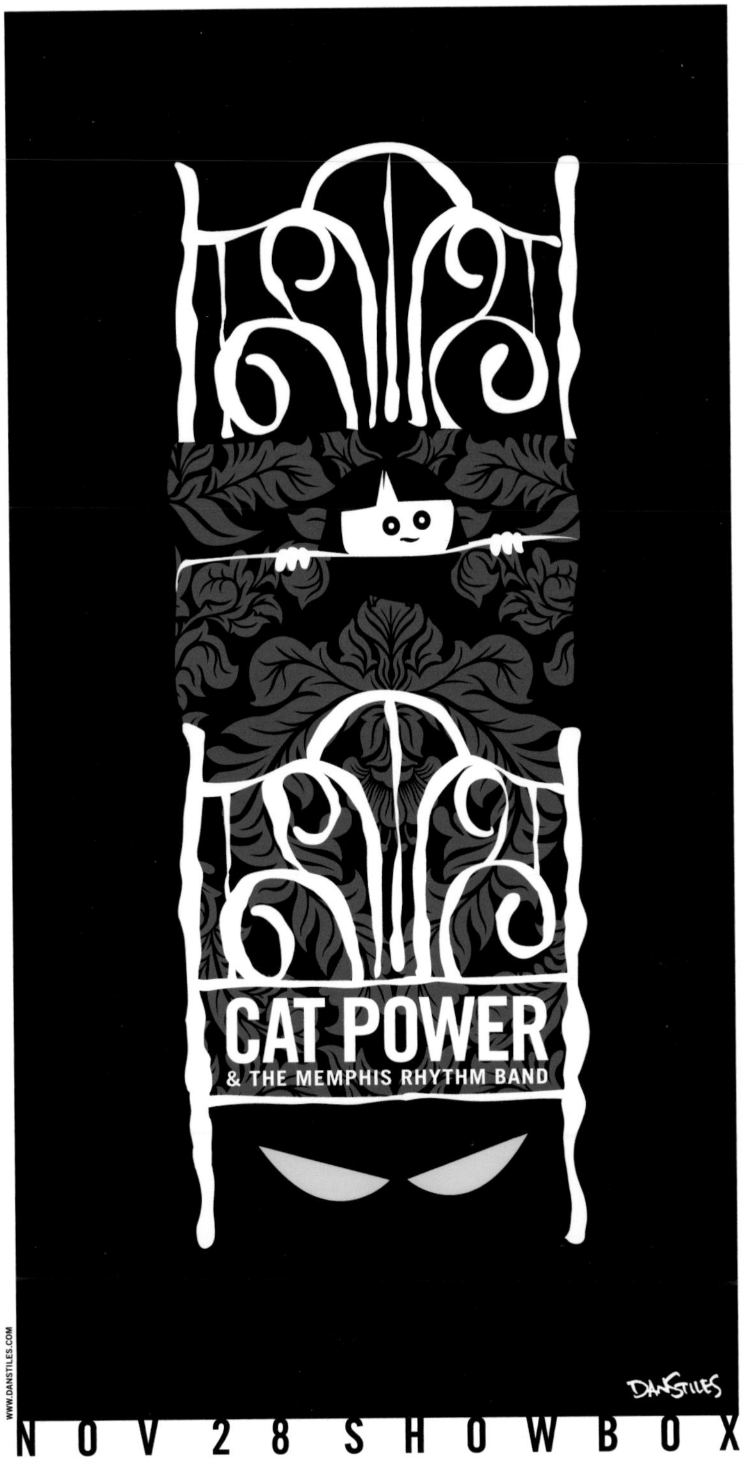

Dan Stiles Cat Power, Decemberists – Posters, 2006 / 2007

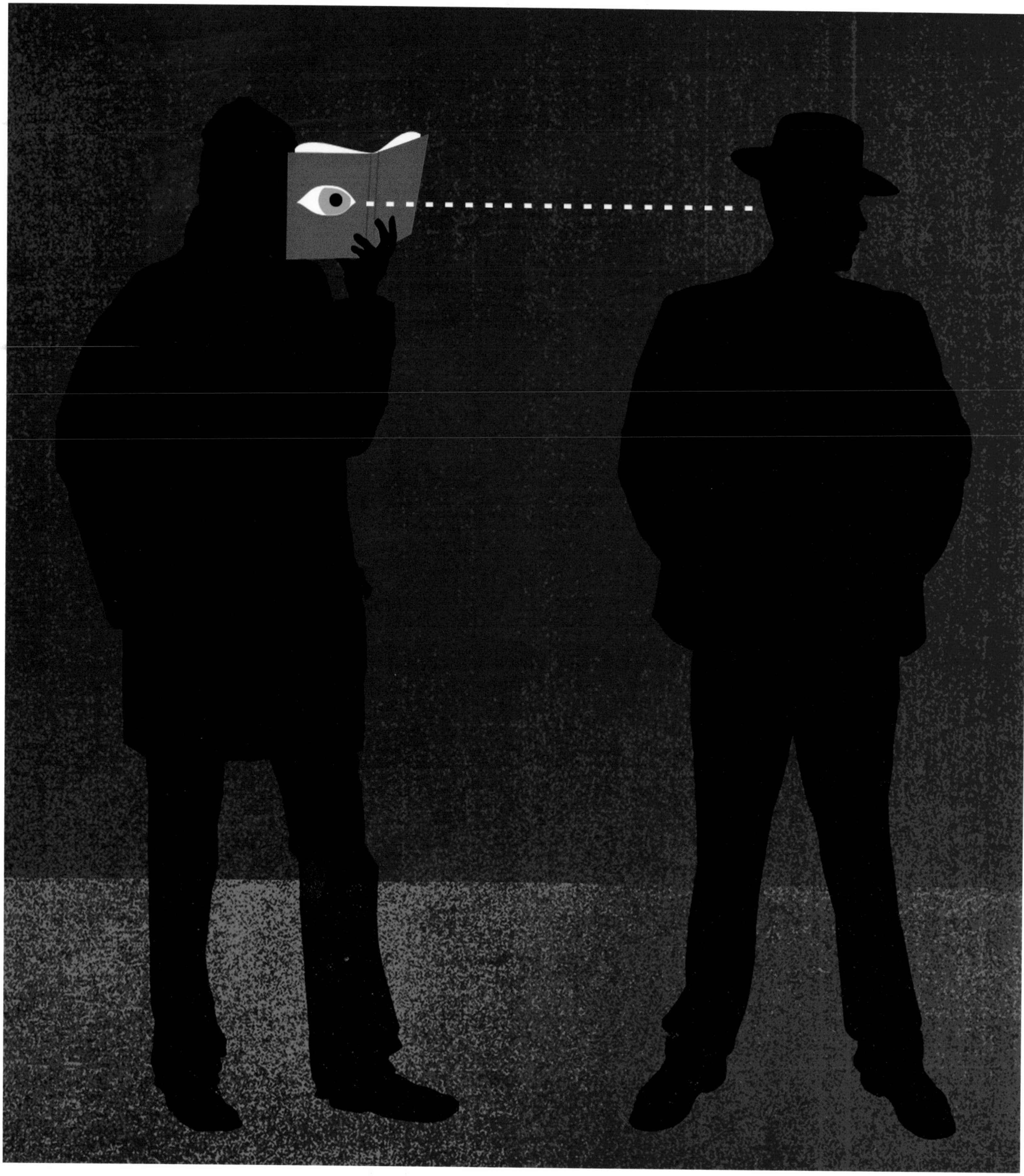

Andrio Abero | 33rpm Spy Books - Editorial, 2008

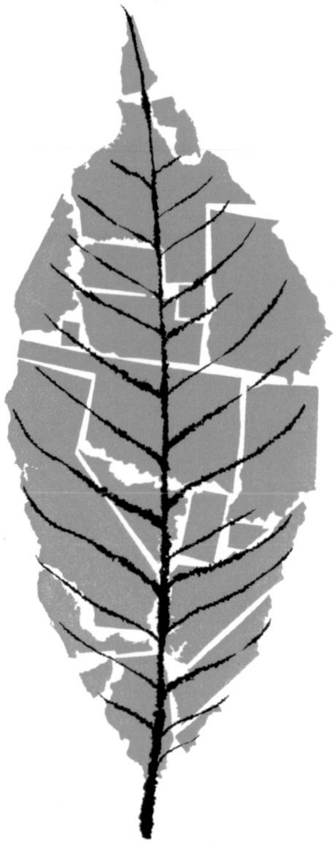

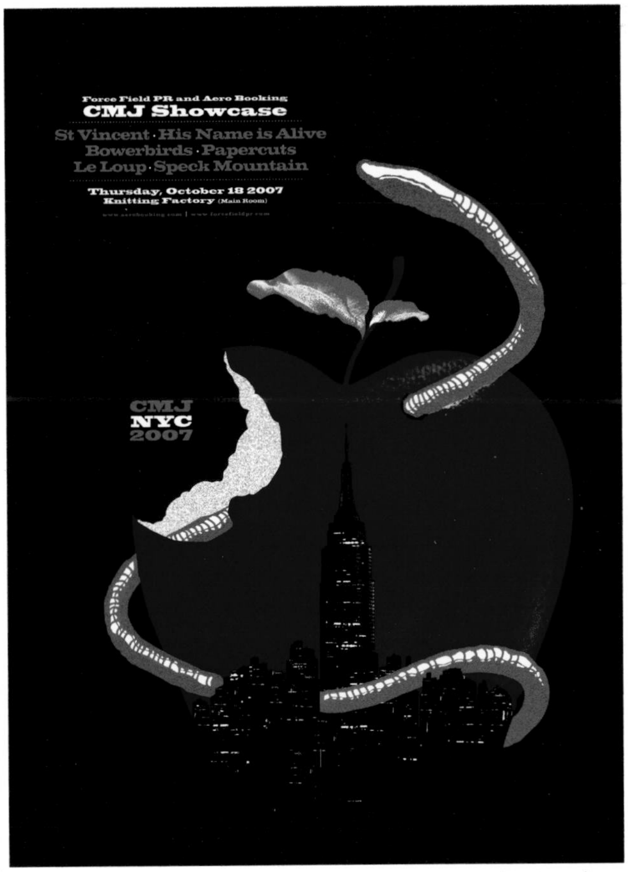

Andrio Abero | 33rpm Free Fall (top), Rufus Wainwright, Aero Booking Showcase – Poster, 2007/2008 **The Heads of State** Green States (top) – Editorial, 2008

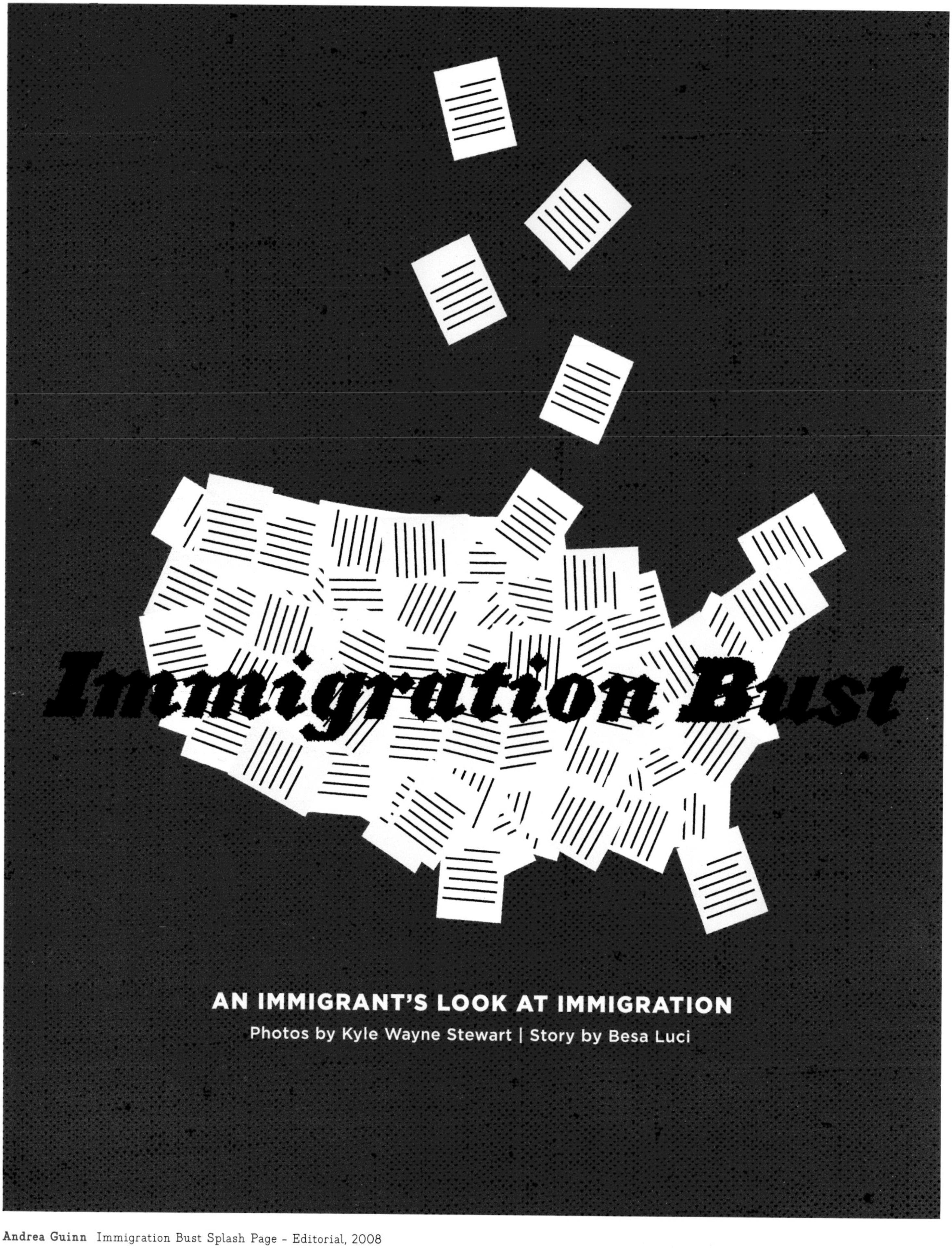
Immigration Bust
AN IMMIGRANT'S LOOK AT IMMIGRATION
Photos by Kyle Wayne Stewart | Story by Besa Luci

Andrea Guinn Immigration Bust Splash Page - Editorial, 2008

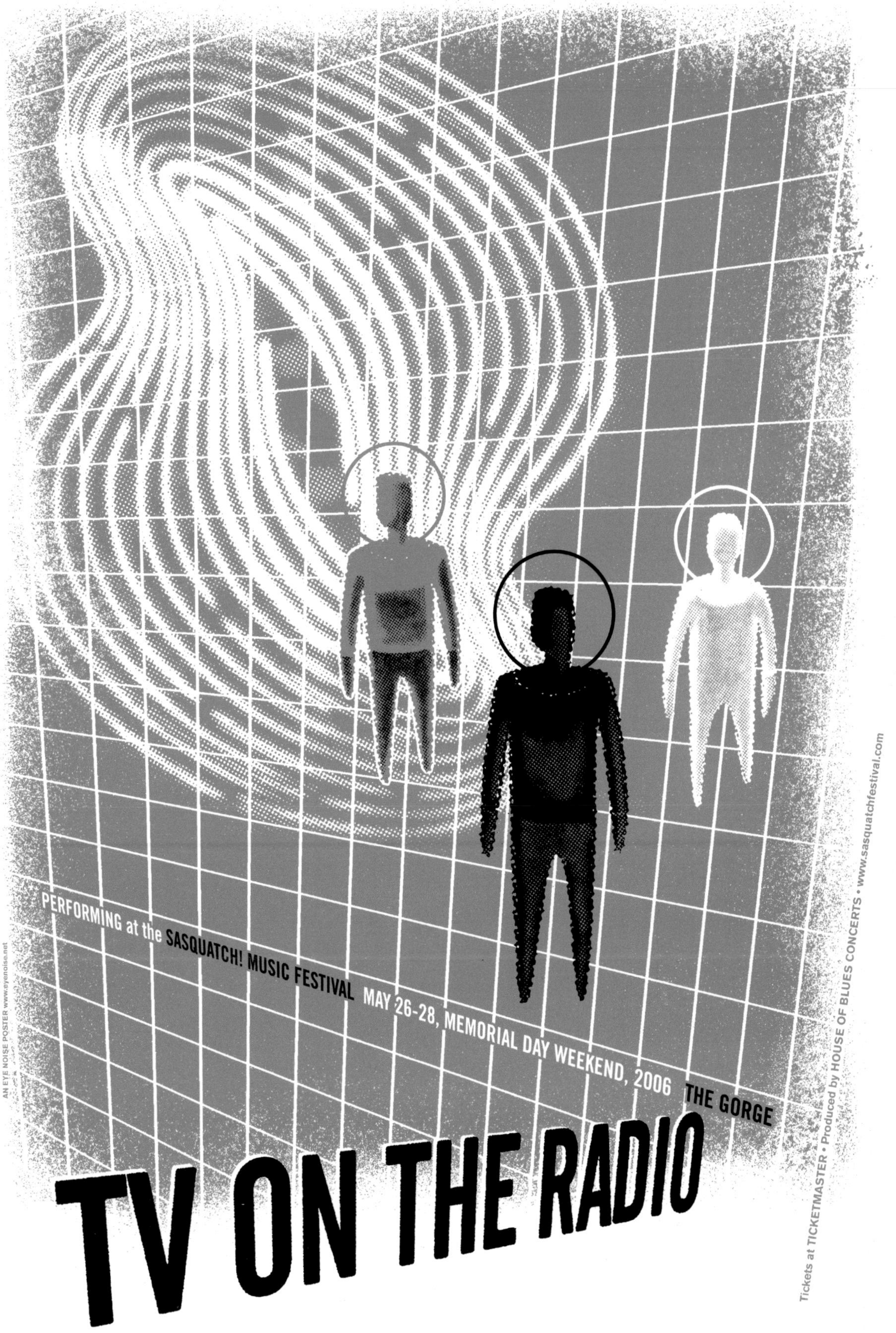
PERFORMING at the SASQUATCH! MUSIC FESTIVAL MAY 26-28, MEMORIAL DAY WEEKEND, 2006 THE GORGE
TV ON THE RADIO
AN EYE NOISE POSTER www.eyenoise.net
Tickets at TICKETMASTER • Produced by HOUSE OF BLUES CONCERTS • www.sasquatchfestival.com

Eye Noise TV on the Radio - Poster, 2006

SPOON
with
COLD WAR KIDS * AGAINST ME * MUTE MATH
12·04·2007
The Roxy, Boston, Massachusetts

Strawberryluna Spoon - Poster, 2007

Strawberryluna Winter - Art Print, 2008

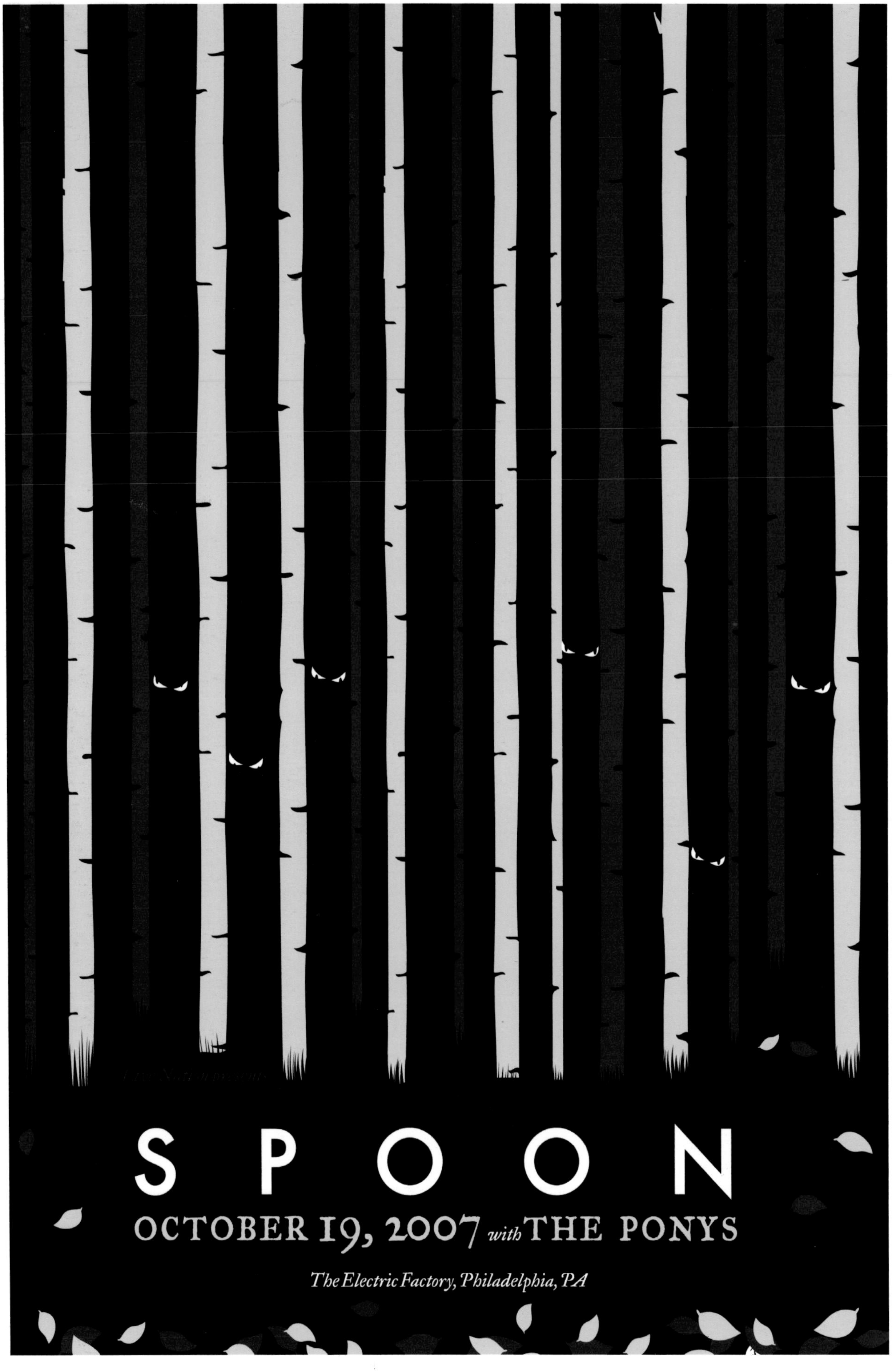
SPOON
OCTOBER 19, 2007 with THE PONYS
The Electric Factory, Philadelphia, PA

Strawberryluna Spoon - Poster, 2007

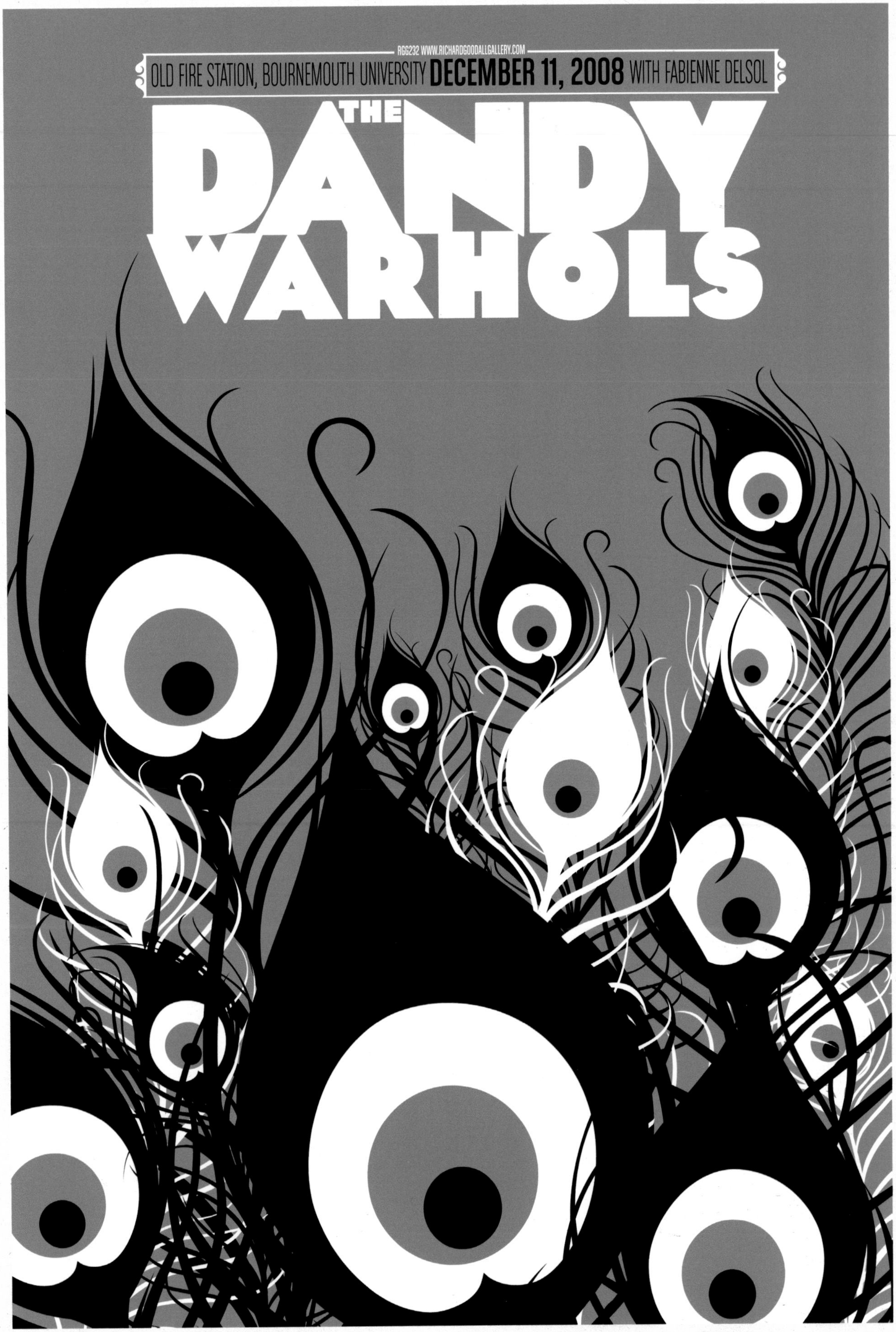
RGG232 WWW.RICHARDGOODALLGALLERY.COM
OLD FIRE STATION, BOURNEMOUTH UNIVERSITY DECEMBER 11, 2008 WITH FABIENNE DELSOL
THE
DANDY
WARHOLS

Strawberryluna The Dandy Warhols - Poster, 2008

Todd Slater Of Montreal, Jack Johnson – Poster, 2007

The
DECEMBERISTS
12 FEBRUARY 2007 · PRIME CLUB · KOLN, GERMANY

Todd Slater The Decemberists - Poster, 2007

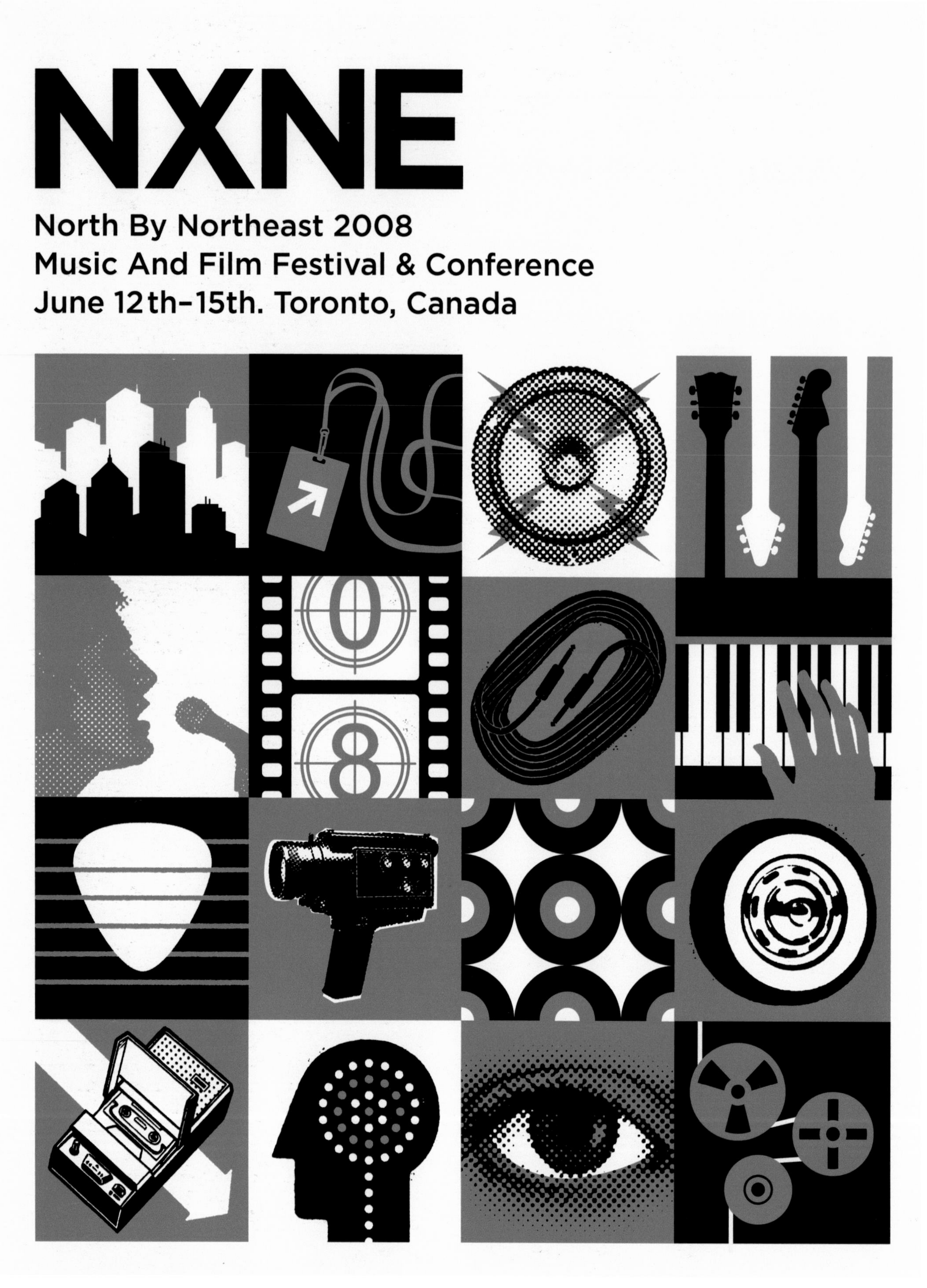

Doublenaut NXNE – Poster, 2008

Human Empire Hope and Fear – Art Print, 2008

Tad Carpenter Lovely - Art Print, 2008 **Doublenaut** Sam Roberts Band, Boris - Poster, 2007/2008

Tad Carpenter Fun Time – Art Print, 2008

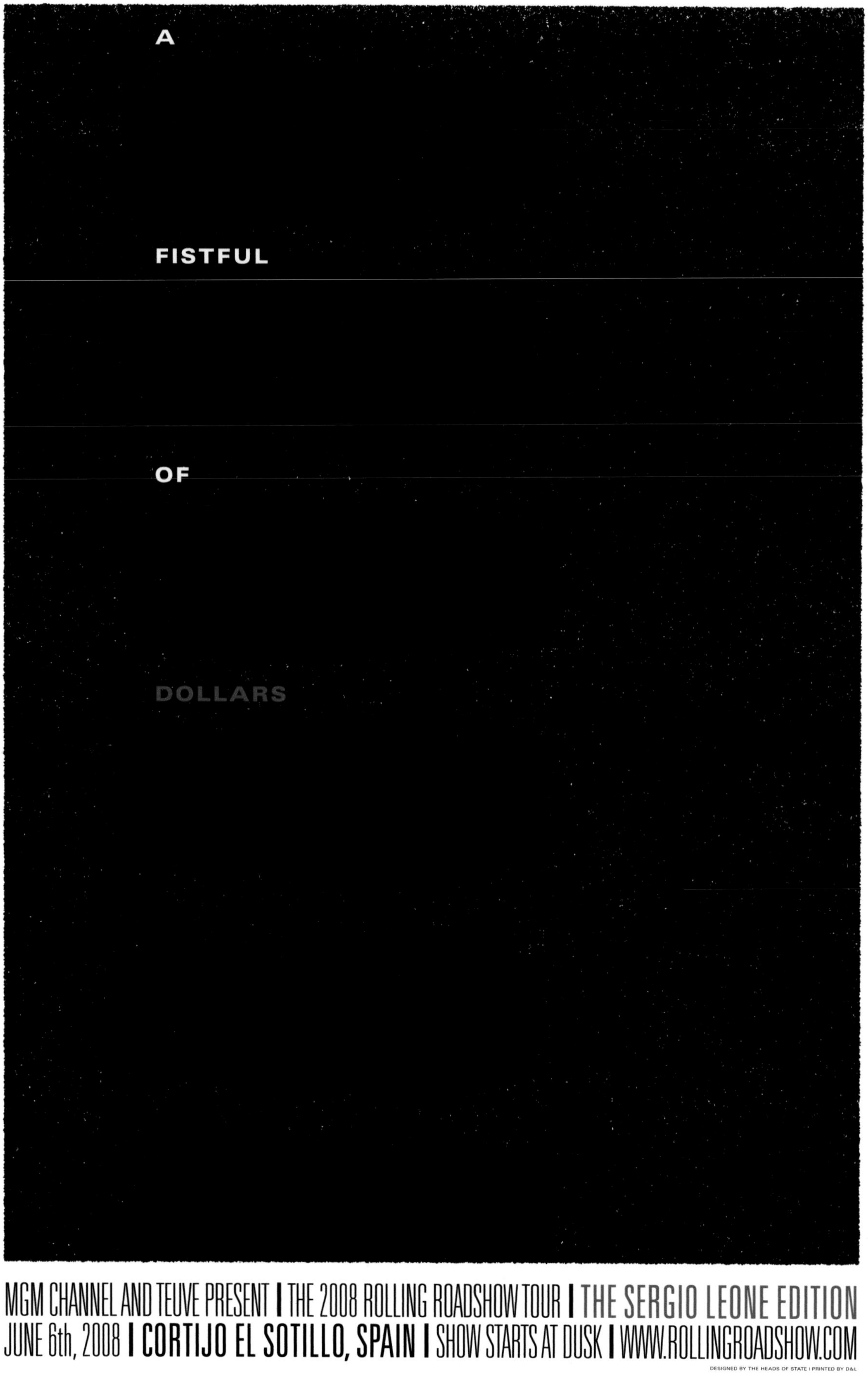
A
FISTFUL
OF
DOLLARS
MGM CHANNEL AND TEUVE PRESENT | THE 2008 ROLLING ROADSHOW TOUR | THE SERGIO LEONE EDITION
JUNE 6th, 2008 | CORTIJO EL SOTILLO, SPAIN | SHOW STARTS AT DUSK | WWW.ROLLINGROADSHOW.COM
DESIGNED BY THE HEADS OF STATE | PRINTED BY D&L

The Heads of State Fistful of Dollars - Poster, 2008

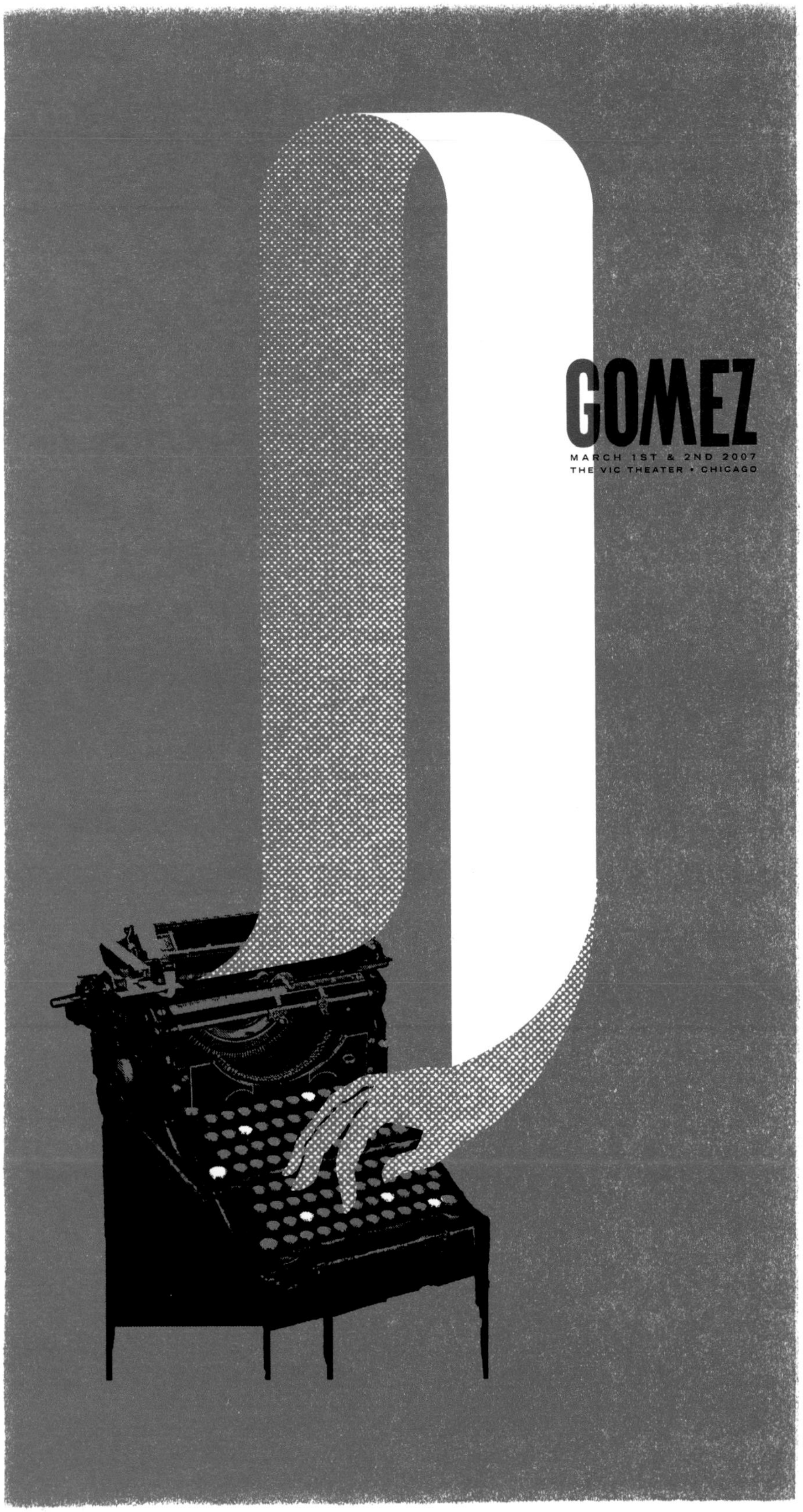

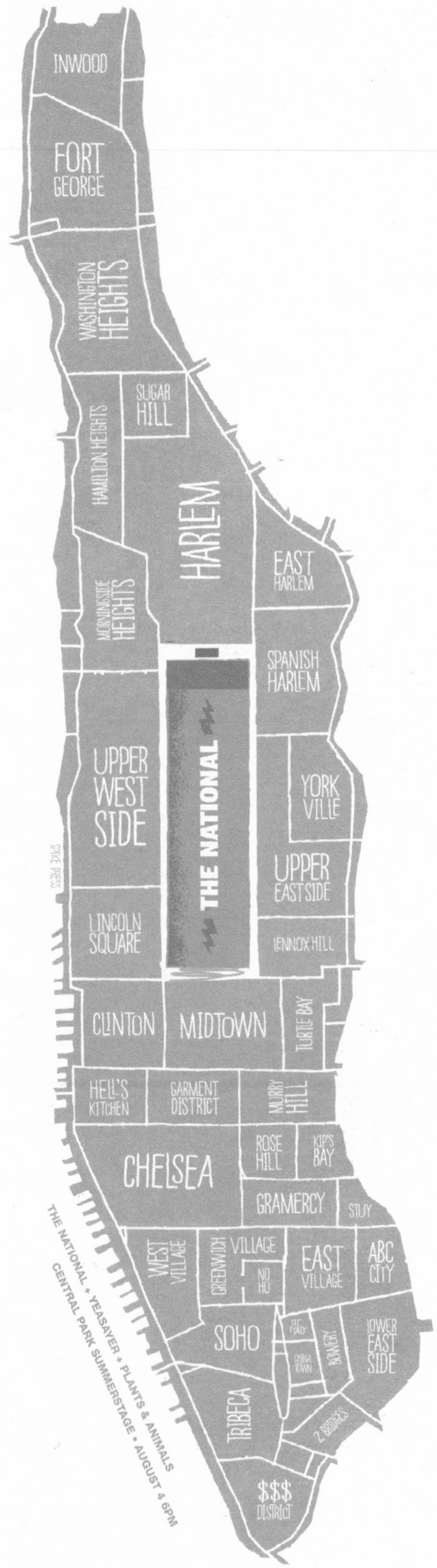

The Heads of State Gomez – Poster, 2007 **Spikepress** The National Central Park – Poster, 2008

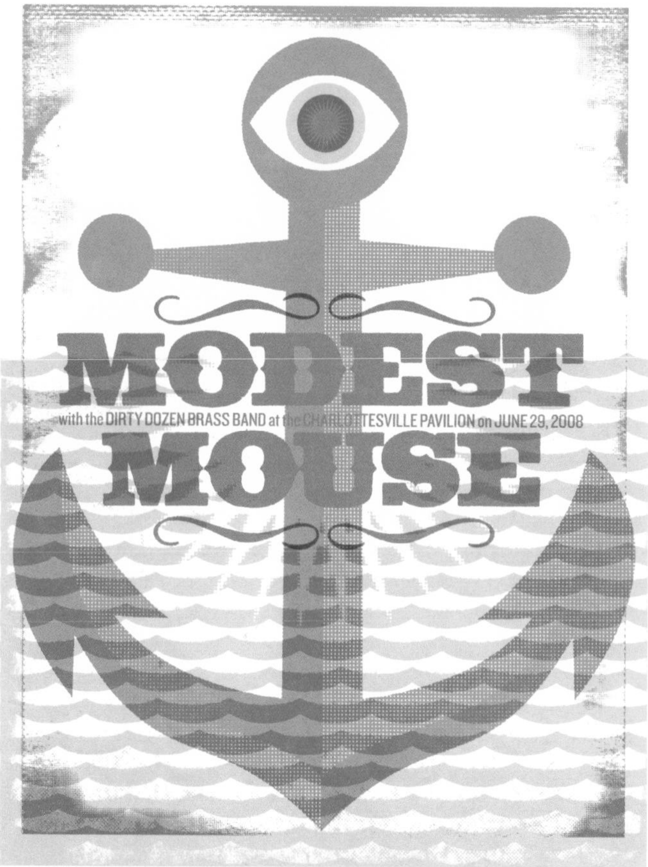

Public Domain Rogue Wave, Modest Mouse, Wilco – Posters, 2007/2008 **Andrio Abero | 33rpm** The New Republic – Editorial, 2006

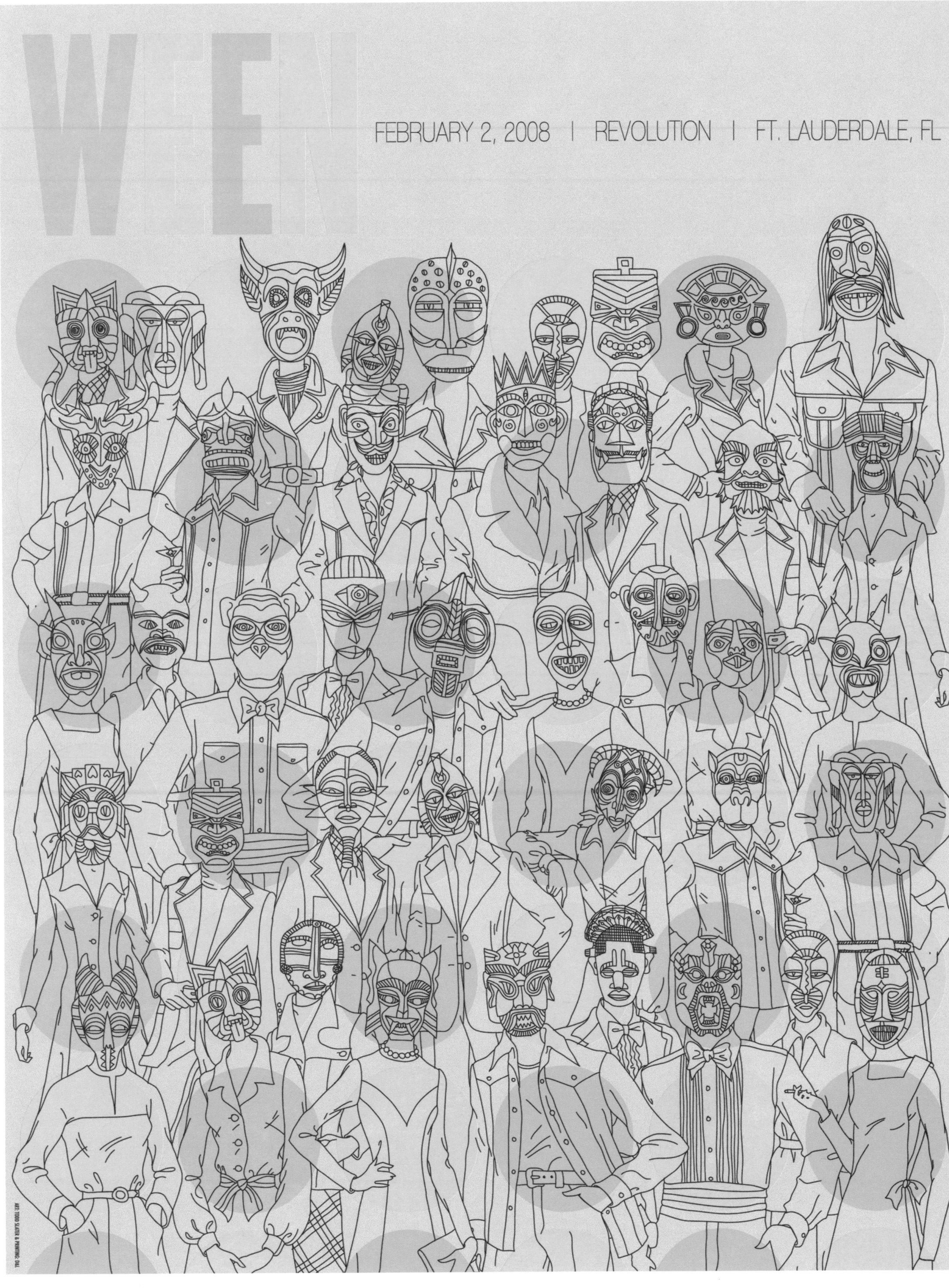
WEEN
FEBRUARY 2, 2008 | REVOLUTION | FT. LAUDERDALE, FL

Todd Slater Ween - Poster, 2007

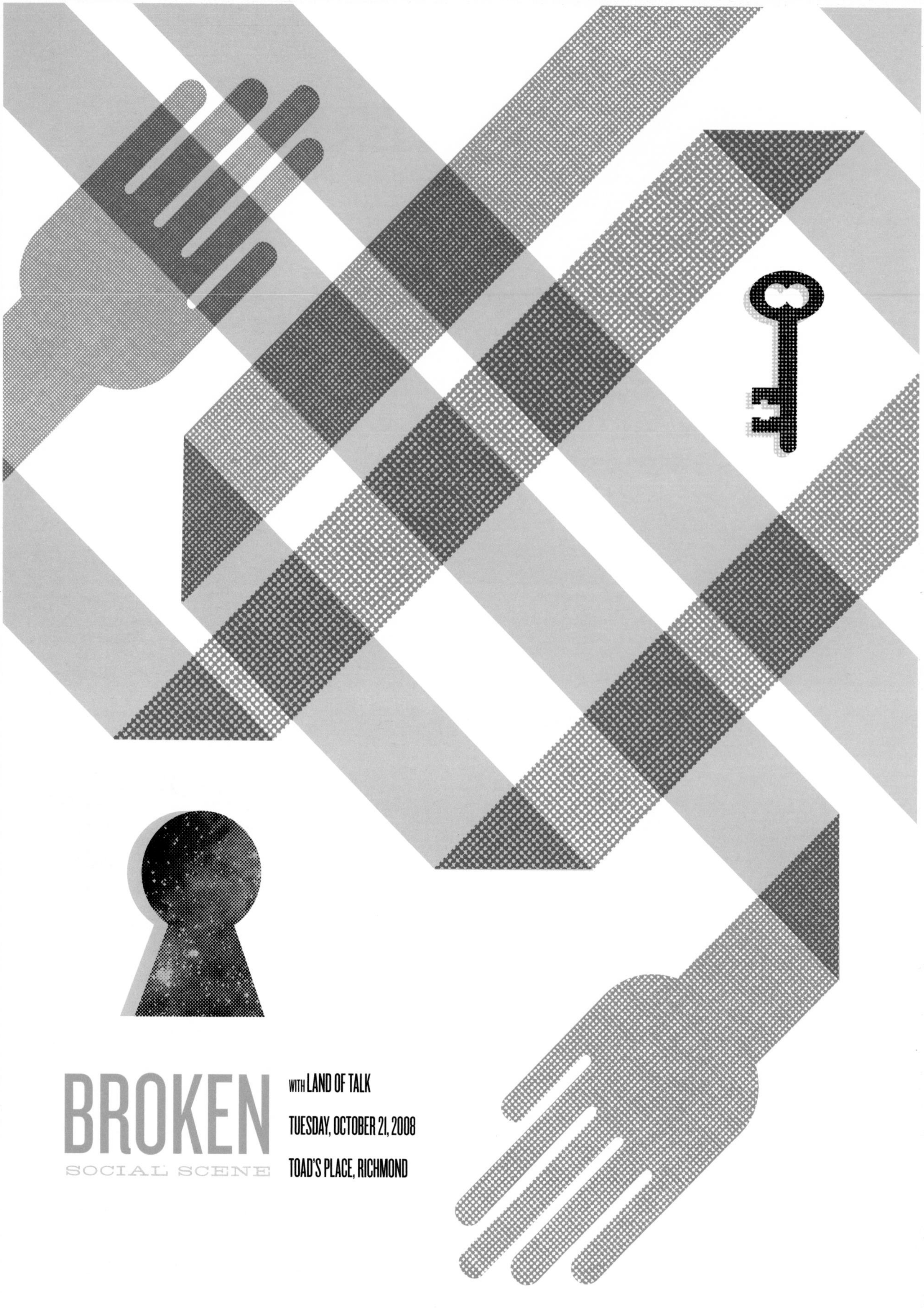

Public Domain Broken Social Scene – Poster, 2008

STARS

WITH
JENNY WHITELEY
November
WEDNESDAY
26
2008
BRONSON
CENTRE
THEATRE
OTTAWA
7
PM
ALL AGES
$27.50
211 BRONSON AVE.

Doublenaut Stars - Poster, 2008

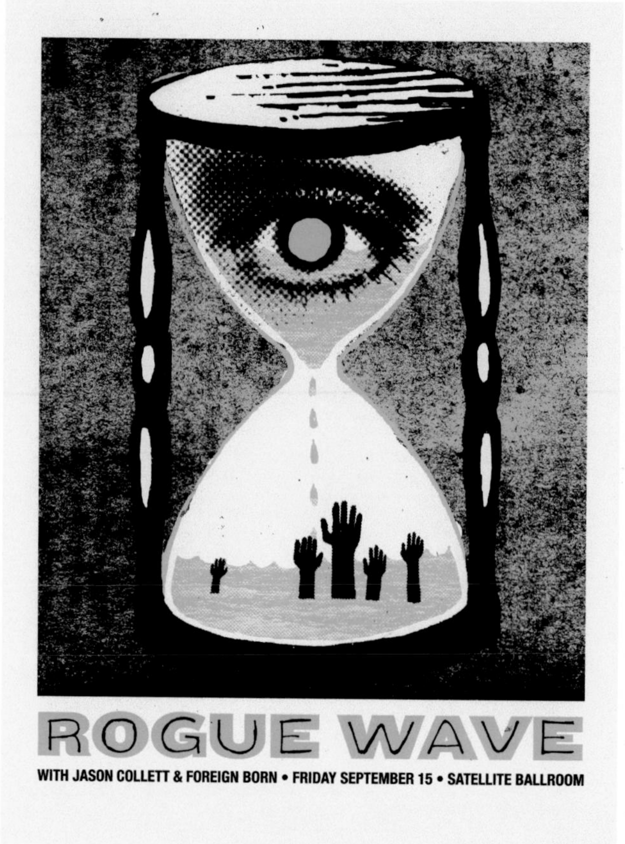

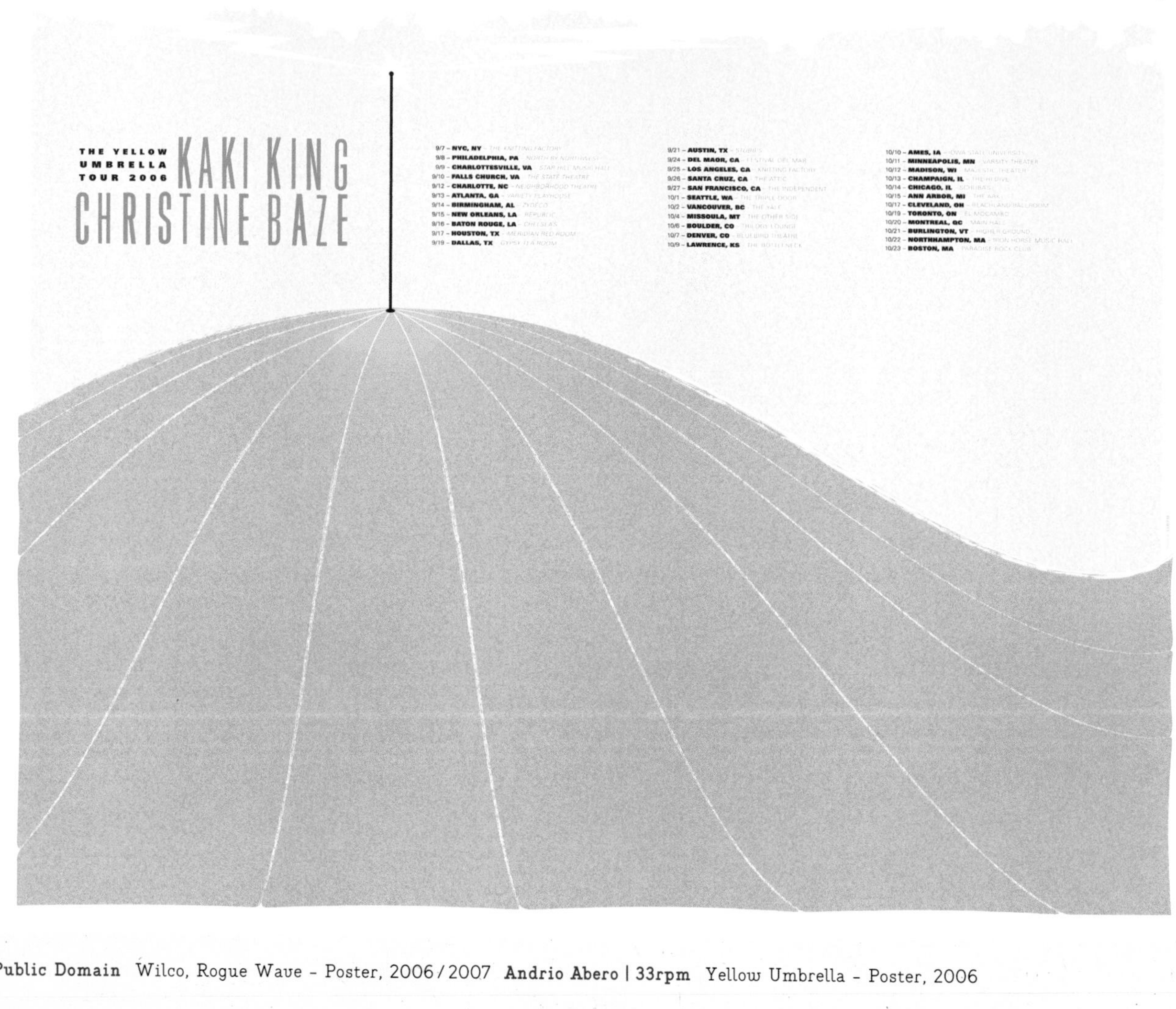

Public Domain Wilco, Rogue Wave – Poster, 2006/2007 **Andrio Abero | 33rpm** Yellow Umbrella – Poster, 2006

POYNTER EYETRACK 2007 PRESENTS:
ENGAGING THE READER
TUESDAY | 30 OCT 2007 | FISHER AUDITORIUM

Andrea Guinn Poynter Institute – Poster, 2007

Pietari Posti GIANTS! Niña - Poster, 2008

Pietari Posti Helsinki Design Week – Magazine Cover, 2008

Pietari Posti GIANTS! Stained Polar Bear – Poster, 2008

Pietari Posti GIANTS! Pulpo – Poster, 2008

Pietari Posti Fashion meets Architecture (left) - Editorial, 2008 ||| Metropolis - Exhibition Poster, 2008

Reintroduce the beast to the wild!
Kinky
Cat
MUSK FOR MEN
YOUNG AT HEART.com
The dating service for senior citizens who believe that age is only a number.

Scotty Reifsnyder Young at Heart: Kinky Cat - Poster, 2007

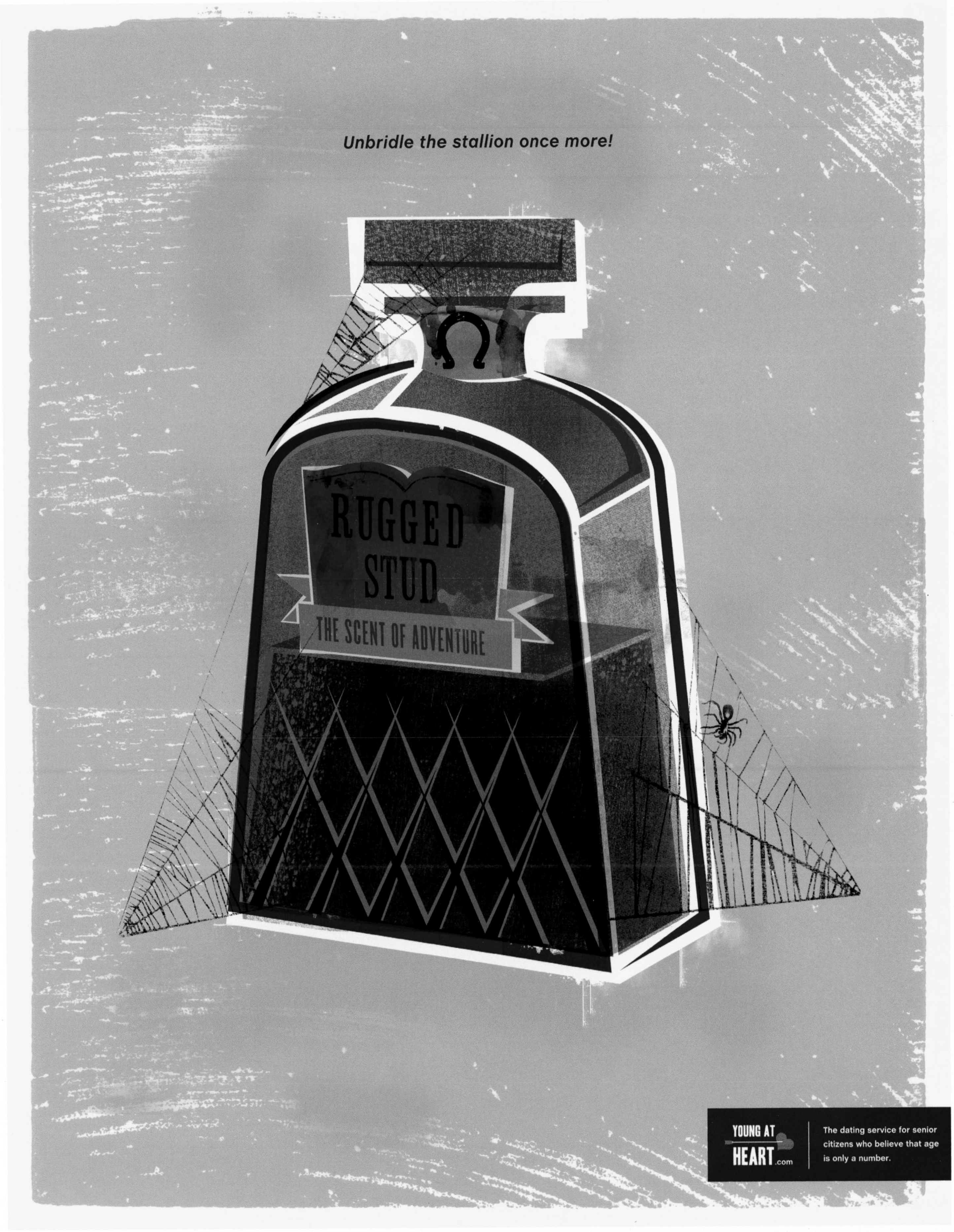
Unbridle the stallion once more!
RUGGED STUD
THE SCENT OF ADVENTURE
YOUNG AT HEART.com
The dating service for senior citizens who believe that age is only a number.

Scotty Reifsnyder Young at Heart: Rugged Stud - Poster, 2007

Get the bunny hopping again!
WHITE RABBIT
EAU DE PARFUM
YOUNG AT HEART.com
The dating service for senior citizens who believe that age is only a number.

Scotty Reifsnyder Young at Heart: White Rabbit – Poster, 2007

DONPERIS
HOLIDAYMUSICSHOW
SATURDAY
DECEMBER15TH
7:30TO10:30PM
PRINCESTREETCAFE
LOCATED AT 15 N. PRINCE ST. IN DOWNTOWN LANCASTER, PENNSYLVANIA.

Scotty Reifsnyder Don Peris Holiday Show – Poster, 2008

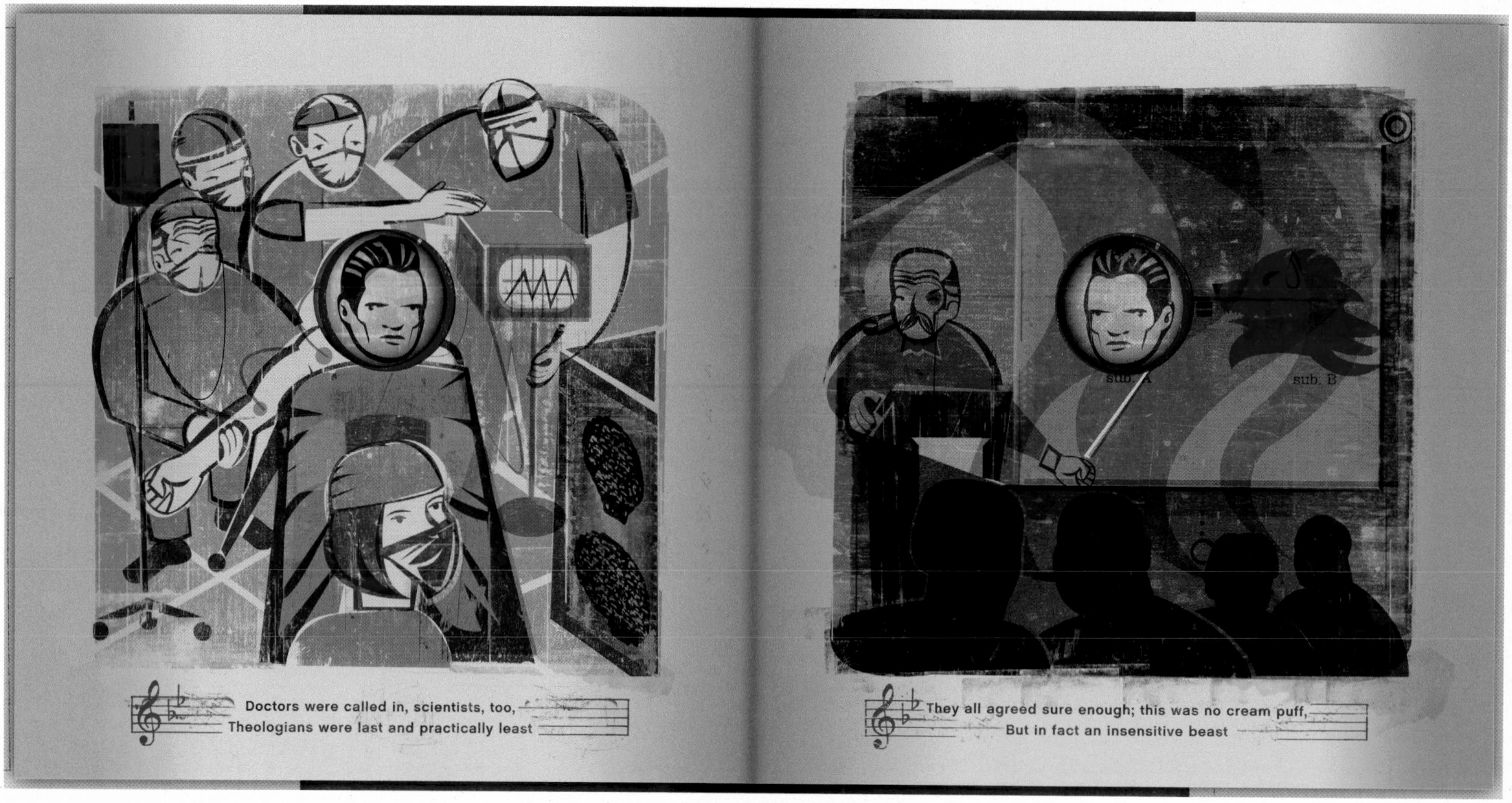
Doctors were called in, scientists, too,
Theologians were last and practically least
sub. A
sub. B
They all agreed sure enough; this was no cream puff,
But in fact an insensitive beast

Sal's
DINER
THE BEST BURGERS IN TOWN
Water and bread was all he was fed,
But not once did a tear stain his face
In jail he was beaten, bullied and buggered,
And was made to make license plates

Scotty Reifsnyder Johnny Cash: The Man Who Couldn't Cry - Children's Book, 2008

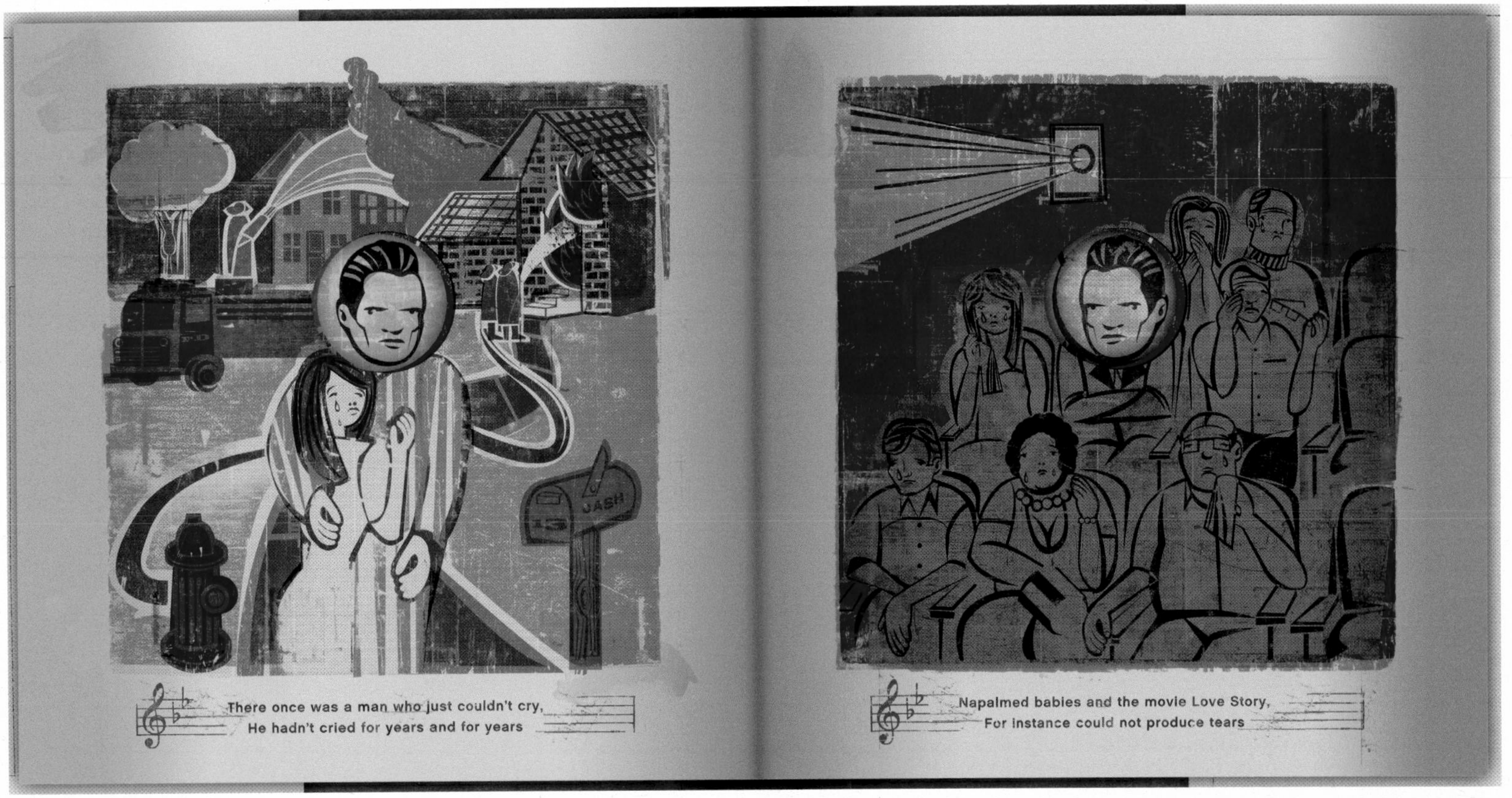
There once was a man who just couldn't cry,
He hadn't cried for years and for years
Napalmed babies and the movie Love Story,
For instance could not produce tears

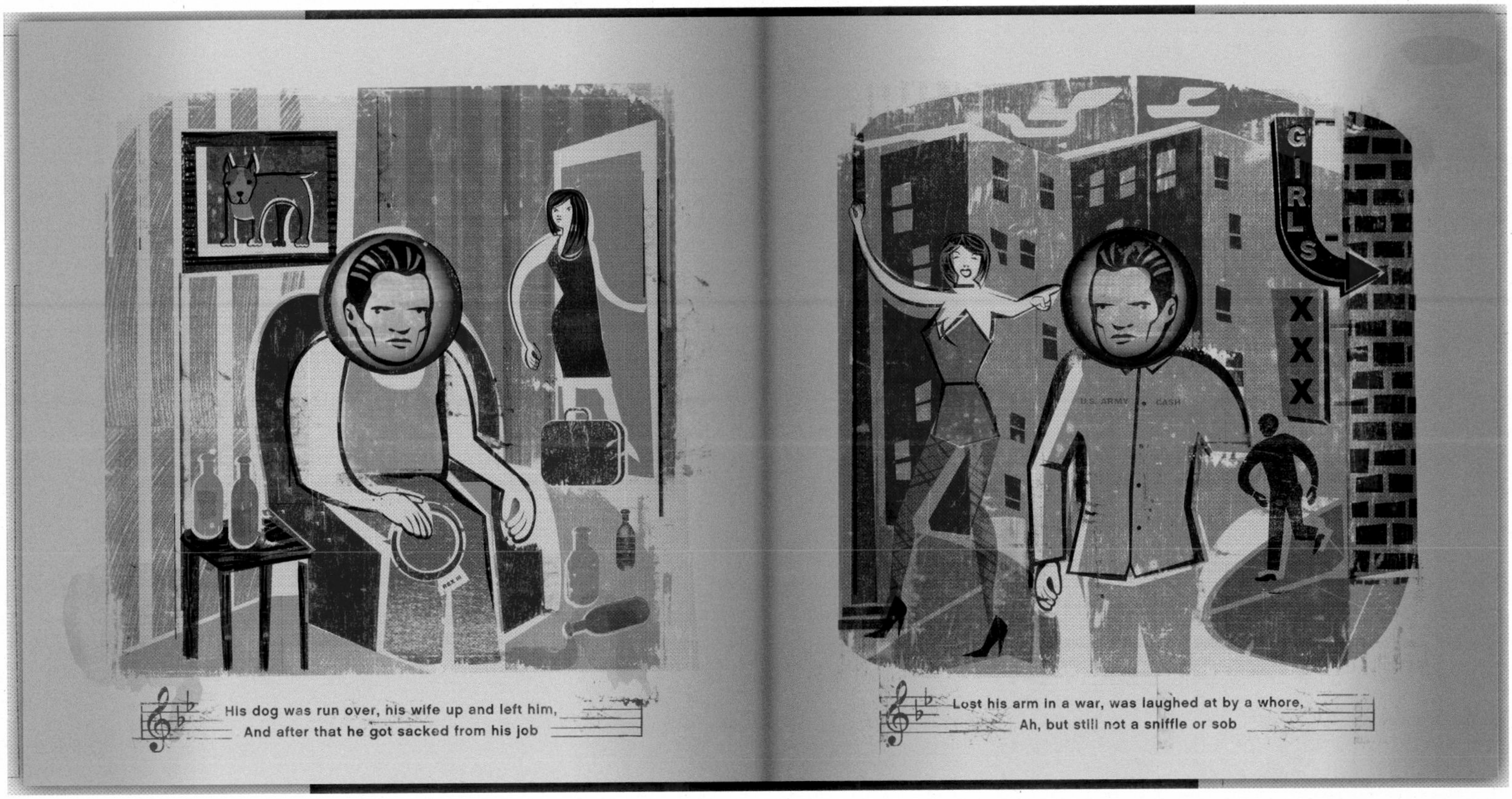
His dog was run over, his wife up and left him,
And after that he got sacked from his job
GIRLS
XXX
Lost his arm in a war, was laughed at by a whore,
Ah, but still not a sniffle or sob

Scotty Reifsnyder Johnny Cash: The Man Who Couldn't Cry – Children's Book, 2008

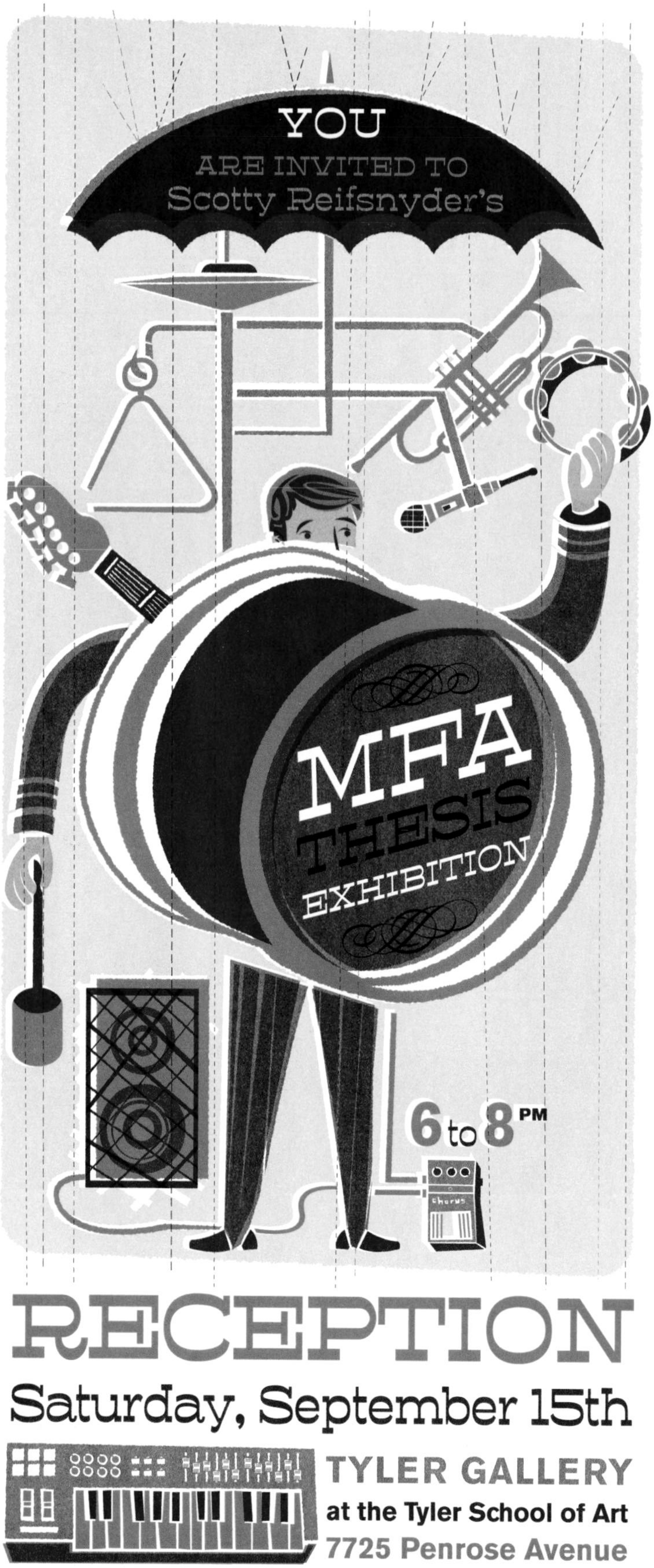
YOU
ARE INVITED TO
Scotty Reifsnyder's
MFA
THESIS
EXHIBITION
6 to 8 PM
RECEPTION
Saturday, September 15th
TYLER GALLERY
at the Tyler School of Art
7725 Penrose Avenue

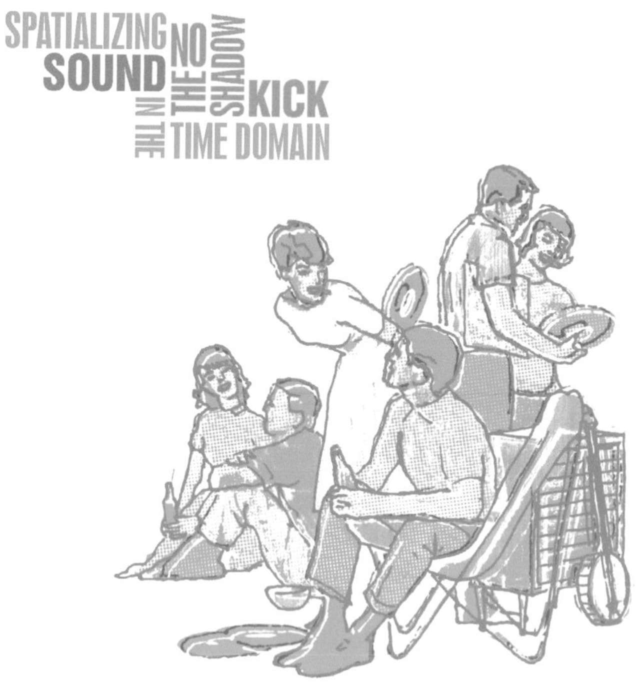
SPATIALIZING SOUND IN THE TIME DOMAIN
NO THE SHADOW KICK

THE NEW
PORNOGRAPHERS
with OKKERVIL RIVER on APRIL 16, 2008
at TOAD'S PLACE, RICHMOND

Scotty Reifsnyder MFA show - Poster, 2007 **Standard Design** No-Shadow Kick - Record Sleeve, 2005 **Public Domain** New Pornographers - Poster, 2008

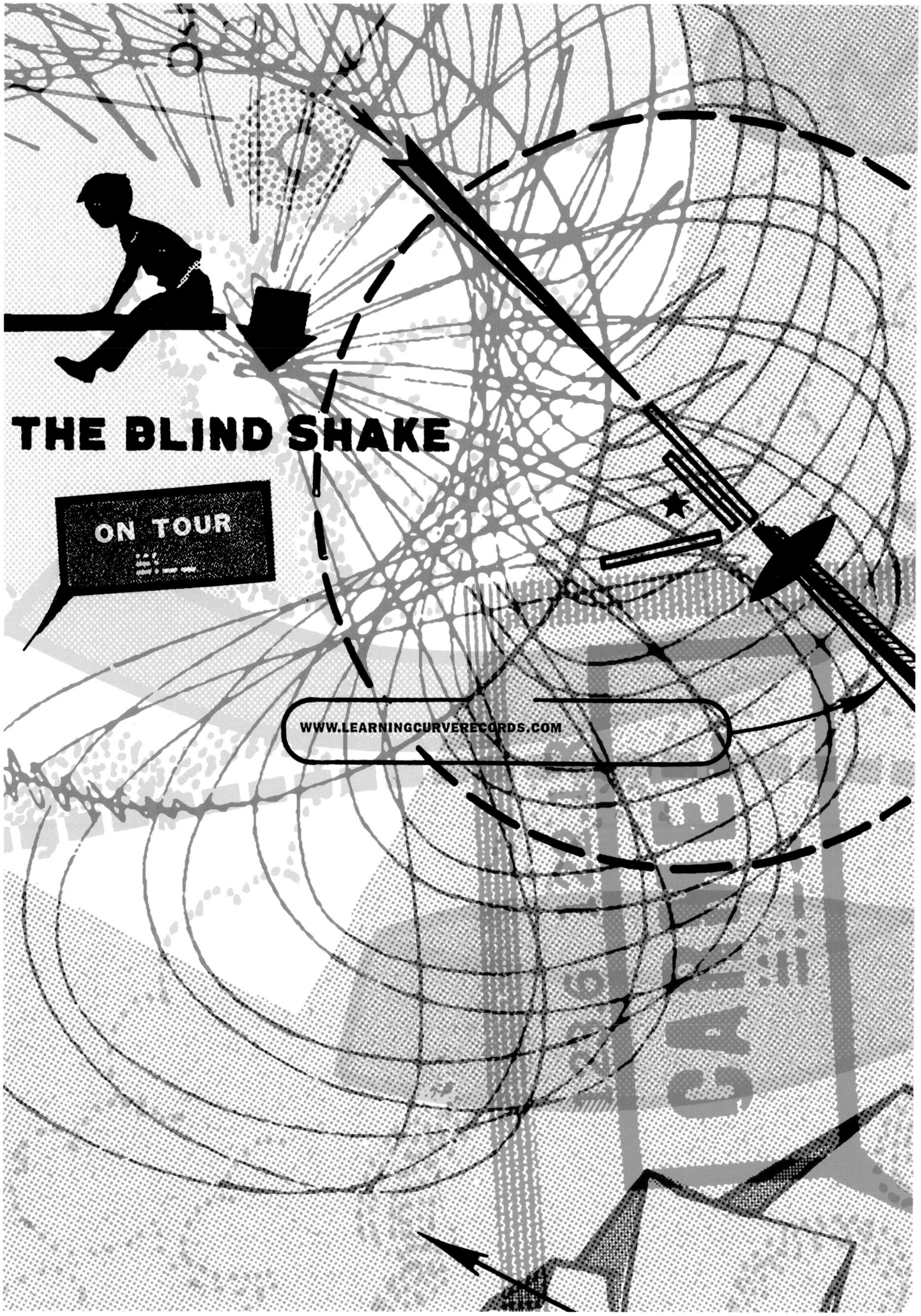

Amy Jo The Blind Shake - Poster, 2008

BUFFALO KiLLERS
FALL TOUR 2007
ALIVE RECORDS

Amy Jo Buffalo Killers - Poster, 2007

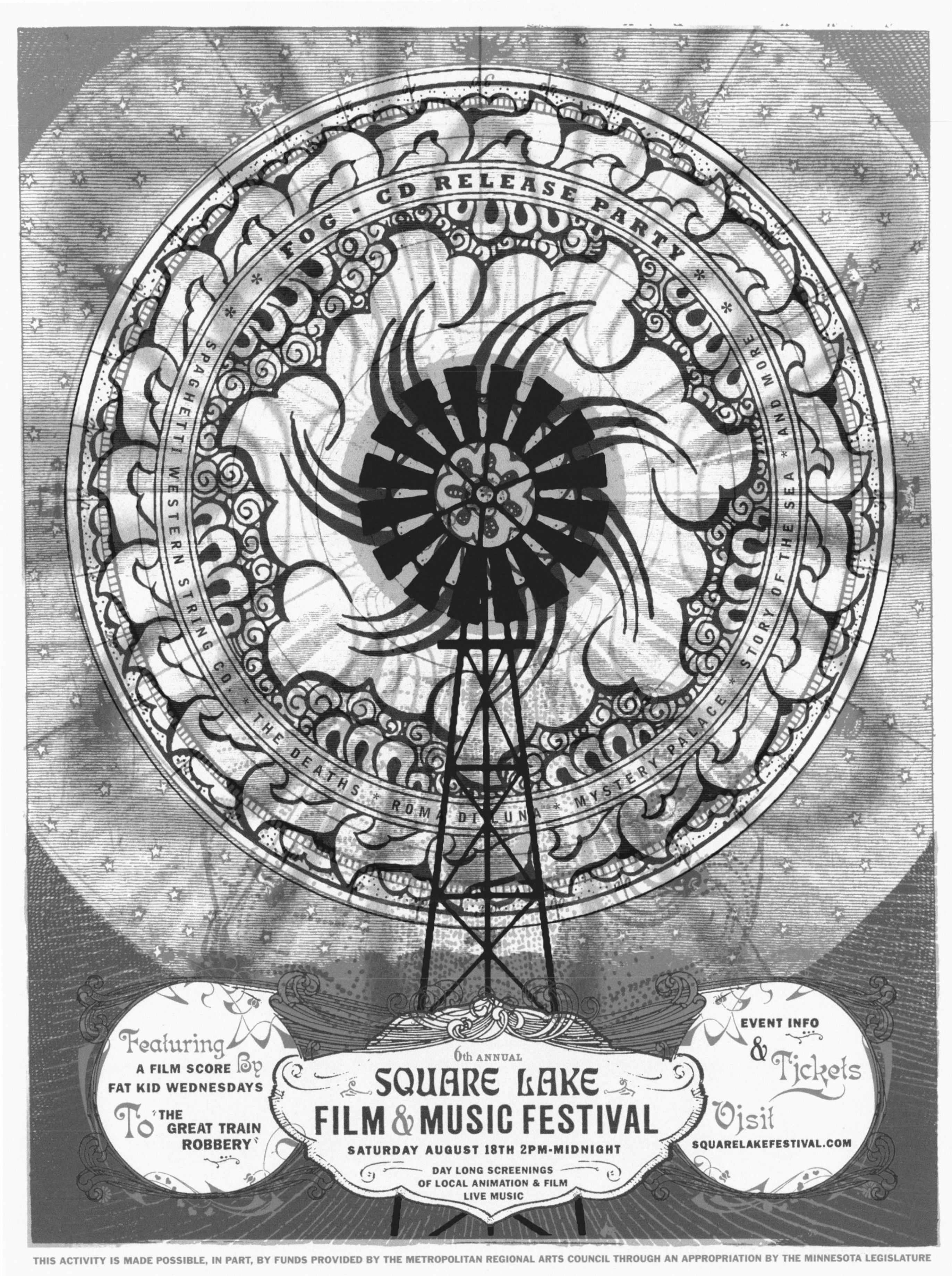
FOG - CD RELEASE PARTY
SPAGHETTI WESTERN STRING CO. * THE DEATHS * ROMA DI LUNA * MYSTERY PALACE * STORY OF THE SEA * AND MORE
Featuring A FILM SCORE By FAT KID WEDNESDAYS To "THE GREAT TRAIN ROBBERY"
6th ANNUAL
SQUARE LAKE
FILM & MUSIC FESTIVAL
SATURDAY AUGUST 18TH 2PM-MIDNIGHT
DAY LONG SCREENINGS OF LOCAL ANIMATION & FILM
LIVE MUSIC
EVENT INFO & Tickets Visit
SQUARELAKEFESTIVAL.COM
THIS ACTIVITY IS MADE POSSIBLE, IN PART, BY FUNDS PROVIDED BY THE METROPOLITAN REGIONAL ARTS COUNCIL THROUGH AN APPROPRIATION BY THE MINNESOTA LEGISLATURE

Amy Jo Square Lake Festival - Poster, 2007

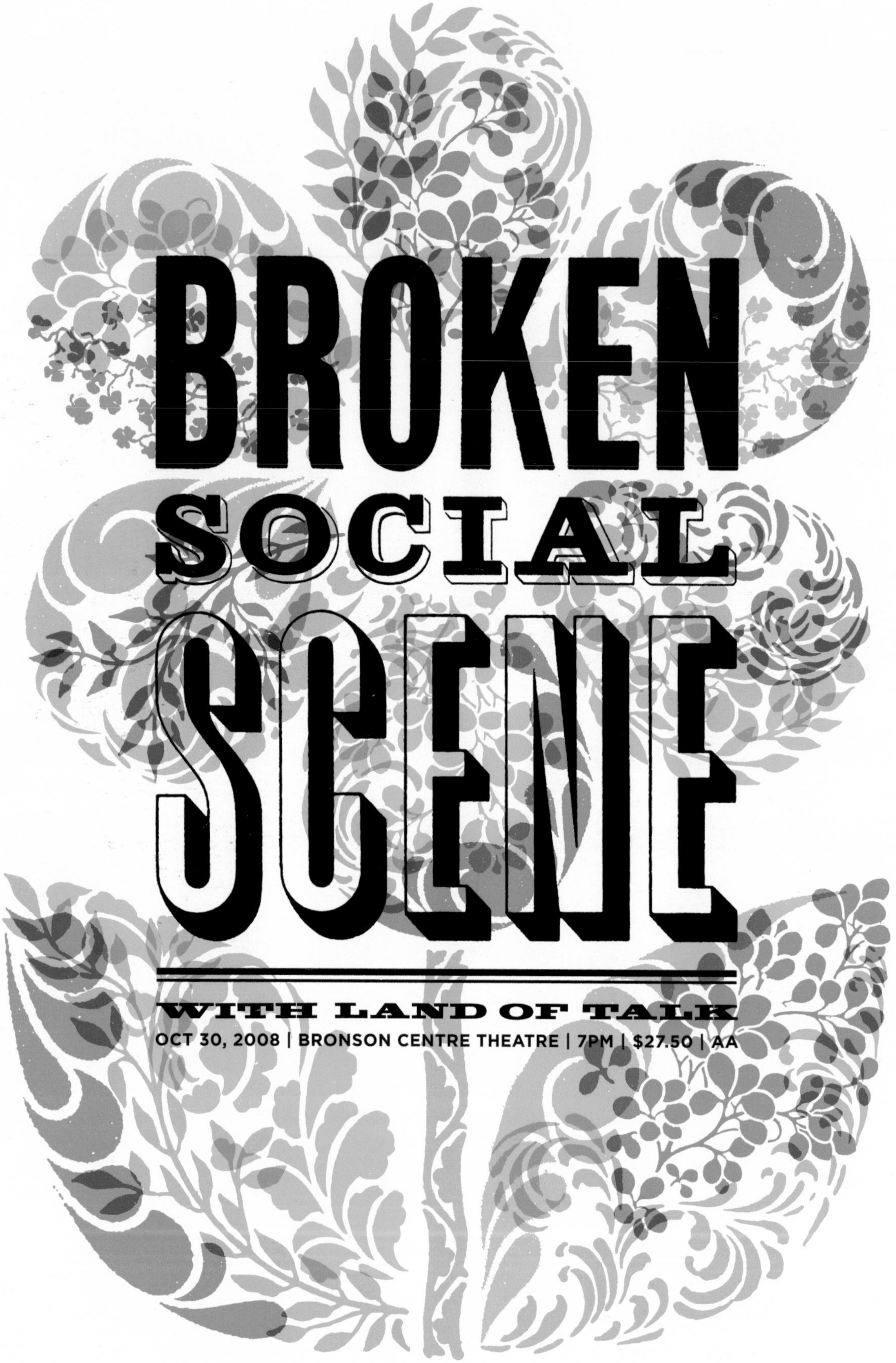
BROKEN
SOCIAL
SCENE
WITH LAND OF TALK
OCT 30, 2008 | BRONSON CENTRE THEATRE | 7PM | $27.50 | AA

Doublenaut Broken Social Scene - Poster, 2008

Pietari Posti Escape – Book Illustration, 2008

Siggi Odds Lundi/Puffin, 2008

Siggi Odds Northwest Coast Self Portrait, Nang Jáadaas Exhibition – Art Prints, 2008

Pietari Posti The Beginning (left) - Editorial, 2007 **Nate Williams** Tin Cup Serenade (top) - Record Sleeve / Poster, 2007

Nate Williams Lion Dress - Personal, 2008

Nate Williams Dreams - Textile Design, 2005

ART POP
FUCK DANCE LET'S ART!
A COLLABORATION WITH LE MUSÉE D'ART CONTEMPORAIN DE MONTRÉAL
RODNEY GRAHAM BAND
EXHIBITIONS / CURATED:
CHARLES BURNS
JOHN VAN HAMERSVELD
ARTPOPMONTREAL.COM

Seripop Art Pop Festival (left) - Poster, 2006 ||| Gothik Thursday - Flyer, 2008

Nate Williams Letter Life - Personal, 2008

Nate Williams His and Hers - Personal, 2008

Nate Williams Cervical Awareness – Textile Design, 2008

Matte Stephens Do-Nothing Bird / Do-Nothing - Painting, 2007

Josh Cochran 100 Hundred Cars (2) - Editorial, 2006

Josh Cochran 100 Hundred Cars (5) - Editorial, 2006

A-Side Studio
United Kingdom
www.a-sidestudio.co.uk
contact@a-sidestudio.co.uk
80 TK1 - DVD Packaging, 2008
Client: Awen Productions

Adrian Johnson
United Kingdom
www.adrianjohnson.co.uk
info@adrianjohnson.org.uk
63 Resistance is Fertile - T-Shirt / Poster, 2008 | Client: PartOfIt.org
Memories, Answers, Make your point - Poster, 2008 | Client: Giant Robot

Amy Jo
USA
www.missamyjo.com
hey@missamyjo.com
96 The Trashmen - Poster, 2008 | Client: The Turf Club
100 Thrushes / Glasvegas, Buffalo Killers - Posters, 2007
153 The Blind Shake - Poster, 2008 | Client: Learning Curve Records
154 Buffalo Killers - Poster, 2007
155 Square Lake Festival - Poster, 2007 | Client: Square Lake Productions

Andrea Guinn
USA
http://andreaguinn.com
hello@andreaguinn.com
84 International Orientation - T-Shirt, 2008
Client: University of Missouri
Anywhere But Here - Editorial, 2008 | Client: Vox Magazine
85 Book Signing - Poster, 2008
Client: Stephens Bookshelf (Stephens College)
120 Immigration Bust Splash Page - Editorial, 2008
Client: Vox Magazine
139 Poynter Institute - Poster, 2007 | Client: University of Missouri School of Journalism

Andrio Abero | 33rpm
USA
www.33rpmdesign.com
andrio@33rpmdesign.com
84 Wordless Music Series - Poster, 2007 | Client: New York Society for Ethical Culture
100 Chekhov / Lizardbrain - Poster, 2007 | Client: Pig Iron Theatre
113 The Raveonettes - Poster, 2007
118 Spy Books - Editorial, 2008
Client: FHM Magazine
119 Free Fall - Poster, 2008 | Client: BusinessWeek Magazine
Rufus Wainwright - Poster, 2008 | Client: Seattle Theatre Group
Aero Booking Showcase - Poster, 2007 | Client: Aero Booking
134 The New Republic - Editorial, 2006
138 Yellow Umbrella - Poster, 2006 | Client: Popsmear

Carlos Otalora
Germany
www.tejedor.tv
caminanterojo@gmail.com
30/31 Leichtweber, Madre Selva, Folclor Muisca, Pinta Cielo - Personal, 2008

Chickenbilly
USA
www.chickenbilly.com
billy@chickenbilly.com
72/73 Deer Hunter, Evening Owl, Sea Bat, Captain Mustache, Cold Turkey, Oz Monkey, Flower Beard - Personal, 2008

Chris Haughton
United Kingdom
www.vegetablefriedrice.com
chris@vegetablefriedrice.com
64 Digital Digging - Editorial, 2006 | Client: RES magazine | Credits: Juliette Cezzar
65 Billybag / Fair Trade Handbag - Textile Design, 2007

Dan Stiles
USA
www.publicdomaindesign.com
info@publicdomaindesign.com
22 Feist, Hot Chip, Ted Leo, Jack Johnson - Posters, 2007 / 2008 | Client: Monqui Presents
90 50Foot Wave, Scissor Sisters, Zero 7 - Posters, 2007 / 2008 | Client: Monqui Presents
115 Death Cab for Cutie - Poster, 2008 | Client: AEG LiveNation
117 Cat Power, Decemberists - Posters, 2006 / 2007 | Client: Monqui Presents

Darling Clementine
Norway
www.darlingclementine.no
post@darlingclementine.no
3 Haberdashery Series - Personal, 2006
4/5 Candy Cane Christmas Series - Greeting Cards, 2008
16/17 Nöel Series - Greeting Cards, 2007
Design & Concept: Ingrid Reithaug & Tonje Holand.

Doublenaut
Canada
www.doublenaut.com
info@doublenaut.com
95 Dave Matthews Band - Poster, 2007
100 Pascale Picard - Poster, 2008 | Client: Myspace Canada
101 In the Land of Long Fingernails - Book Cover, 2008 | Client: Penguin Canada
108 Passenger Action - Poster, 2008 | Client: Small Man Records
109 Dave Matthews Band - Poster, 2007
128 NXNE - Poster, 2008 | Client: NXNE
130 Sam Roberts Band, 2007 | Client: Arts & Crafts
Boris - Poster, 2008 | Client: Revolution Rock
137 Stars - Poster, 2008 | Client: Revolution Rock
156 Broken Social Scene - Poster, 2008 | Client: Revolution Rock
Designer: Andrew &/or Matthew McCracken

El Jefe
USA
www.eljefedesign.com
info@eljefedesign.com
42 Sharon Jones and The Dap-Kings - Poster, 2008
Client: The Black Cat
43 My Morning Jacket - Poster, 2008
97 Dean and Britta - Poster, 2008
Client: The Black Cat
111 Magnolia Electric Company - Poster, 2007
Client: The Black Cat
Designer: Jeffrey Everett, Printer: Grand Palace

Eva Mastrogiulio
Argentina
www.hazloquequieras.com.ar
evamas05@gmail.com
82 The Whale - Children's book, 2008

Eye Noise
USA
www.eyenoise.com
thomas@eyenoise.net
106 Iron & Wine - Poster, 2006
113 The Hold Steady - Poster, 2007
114 The Detroit Cobras - Poster, 2007
121 TV on the Radio - Poster, 2006

F2 Design
USA
www.f2-design.com
dirk@f2-design.com
92 The Raconteurs - Poster, 2008
109 Ramblin' Jack Elliott Poster, 2005 | Client: Cactus Cafe
Scott H. Biram - Poster, 2005 | Client: KTXT 88.1

General Pattern
United Kingdom
www.generalpattern.net
james@generalpattern.net
50 Thank You - Art Print, 2007
51 Wave, Flag, Voodoo - Art Prints, 2007/2008
Designer: James Brown

Hanna Werning
Sweden
www.byhanna.com
hello@byhanna.com
47 Tiles - Wallpaper Poster, 2006
49 Cone Shell, Hanna W. - Greeting Cards, 2006/2009
99 Soho Square - Wallpaper, 2008

Helen Dardik
Canada
www.oneluckyhelen.com
dardik@sympatico.ca
24 Mod Friends - Personal, 2007
25 Danish Garden Friends - Personal, 2008
26 Bird House Party - Personal, 2009
27 Bird Parade - Personal, 2008
48 Rainbow Berries - Textile Design, 2007
Surface patterns, © Helen Dardik / Lilla Rogers Studio.

Helen Musselwhite
United Kingdom
www.helenmusselwhite.com
78 Daphne in the Woods, 2008

Hero Design Studio
USA
www.heroandsound.com
hero.design@mac.com
93 Decemberists - Poster, 2007

Human Empire
Germany
www.humanempire.com
post@humanempire.com
69 Populous, The Year Of - Record Sleeves, 2007/2008 | Client: Morr Music
The Horror The Horror - Record Sleeves, 2008 | Client: Tapete Records
129 Hope and Fear - Art Print, 2008
Designer: Jan Kruse

James Gulliver Hancock
Australia
www.jamesgulliverhancock.com
james@jamesgulliverhancock.com
33 Camera Vision - T-Shirt, 2008 | Client: Poketo
American Bird - Personal, 2008
40 Cap In Hand - Editorial, 2008 | Client: Business Review Weekly Magazine Australia
Steinway - Personal, 2008
Josh Pyke - Promo Sticker, 2007 | Client: Island Records

Jenn Ski
USA
www.jennski.com
jennski@jennski.com
6/7, 10/11 Diverse - Art Prints, 2007/2008

Jenny Grigg
Australia
www.jennygrigg.com
jenny@jennygrigg.com
66/67 The Tax Inspector, True History of the Kelly Gang, Illywhacker, My Life As A Fake - Book Cover, 2006 | Book Cover Illustrations. Series of ten for Peter Carey's Backlist | Client: Random House Australia

Jen Skelley
USA
www.jenskelley.com
JenSkelley@yahoo.com
18 Puffer Tail, Sprout, Broccolini - Art Print, 2008
19 Love Birds - Art Print, 2007 | Calendar – 2009

Josh Cochran
USA
www.joshcochran.net
mail@joshcochran.net
170/171 100 Hundred Cars (2 & 5) - Editorial, 2006 | Client: Esquire Russia | Art Director: Ekaterina Furceva

Kari Moden
Sweden
www.karimoden.se
kari@moden.se
56/57 Abstract, Boy & Girl, Nails - Ads, 2008 | Client: J&B Whisky | Agency: Kessels Kramer
61 Look, Hair, Shine Baby, Run Baby - Personal, 2008
62 Dating - Editorial, 2007 | Client: The Guardian Weekend Magazine
Flowers - Ad, 2008 | Client: J&B Whisky | Agency: Kessels Kramer
Love - Playing Card, 2008 | Client: Lascivious

Kate Sutton
United Kingdom
www.katesutton.co.uk
suttonkate@hotmail.com
32 Trees - Ad, 2008 | Client: Mount Franklin Water
33 Birdhouses, 2008 | Client: Roxy
38 In the Woods - Art Print, 2008 | Client: Hello Lucky

Katharina Leuzinger
United Kingdom
www.katleuzinger.com
mail@katleuzinger.com
70/71 Kenzo Christmas - Perfume Packaging, 2007 | Client: Kenzo, Paris
75 Untitled - Personal, 2008

La Boca
UK
www.laboca.co.uk
eatme@laboca.co.uk
58 Tom Tyler - Album Cover, 2005 | Client: DC Records
59 The Conversation - T-Shirt, 2007 | Client: www.sixpack.fr
60 Nightmares On Wax - Record Sleeve, 2008 | Client: Warp Records
Design and Illustration by Scot Bendall

Lexie Sullivan
USA
www.lexiesullivan.com
lexie@lexiesullivan.com
12/13 Diverse - Stationery, 2008

Linzie Hunter
UK
www.linziehunter.co.uk
linzie@linziehunter.co.uk
107 Coney - Personal, 2008

Lucy Clark
United Kingdom
www.lucyclarkdesign.com
clarklucy2003@yahoo.co.uk
8 Connect 2, Making tracks 1 & 2, Sliced, Mini Chess, Caged - Textile Design, 2007
9 Disco - Textile Design, 2007
BA textile design course | Degree show: Galashiels London

Marcus Walters
United Kingdom
www.marcuswalters.com
studio@marcuswalters.com
54/55 Abstract (diverse), House, Forest-1, Birds-3 - Personal, 2006/2008
60 Summer, Autumn - Personal, 2005

Matte Stephens
USA
www.matteart.blogspot.com
matteart@gmail.com
20 Portland - Painting, 2008
21 Boston, New Orleans, Family Vacation - Paintings, 2008
169 Do-Nothing Bird / Do-Nothing - Painting, 2007

Matt W. Moore
USA
http://mwmgraphics.com
matt@mwmgraphics.com
52/53 BITNB #1 & #3 - T-Shirt, 2008 | Client: Blood is the new black

Methane
USA
www.methanestudios.com
mark@methanestudios.com
88 Jay Farrar - Poster, 2004 | Client: Echo Lounge
91 Sharon Jones Legs - Poster, 2008 | Client: Ok Productions
96/97 Silver JewsBand of Horses - Posters, 2005 - 2007 | Client: Ok Productions

Nate Duval
USA
www.nateduval.com
nate@nateduval.com
19 Hootie - Art Print, 2008
39 Nighttime in the City - Art Print, 2009
99 Doodle - Art Print, 2008
98 Explosions in the Sky - Poster, 2008 Client: Constant Artists/Explosions in the Sky

Nate Williams
Argentina
www.n8w.com
art@magnetreps.com
168 Cervical Awareness - Textile Design, 2008 | Client: iRoo (Taiwan) | Director: Karina Liu
163 Dreams - Textile Design, 2005 | Graphic for handbag & accesories | Client: Crease
167 His and Hers - Personal, 2008
166 Letter Life - Personal, 2008
162 Lion Dress - Personal, 2008
161 Tin Cup Serenade - Record Sleeve/Poster, 2007 Art Director: Rolf Wilkinson

Nod Young
China
www.behance.net/NodYoung
nod@khakicreative.com
23 The Puti Trees - Personal, 2006

Patent Pending Industries
USA
www.patentpendingindustries.com
info@patentpendingindustries.com
104 Sleater-Kinney - Poster, 2005
The Good, the Bad & the Ugly - Poster, 2008 | Client: Alamo Drafthouse and Cinema
Iron & Wine/Calexico - Poster, 2005 | Client: House of Blues
105 Decemberists - Poster, 2007 | Client: Goodall Gallery / Decemberists
106 Bright Eyes - Poster, 2004
109 Godfather - Poster, 2009
Illustration by Jeff Kleinsmith &/or Jesse LeDoux

Peach Beach
Germany
www.peachbeach.de
info@peachbeach.de
74 The Face Tattoo - T-Shirt, 2008 | Client: Scribtee
81 Timberland - T-Shirt, 2008 | Client: Threadless
83 You don't need vehicles to move something! - Poster, 2008

Pietari Posti
Spain
www.pposti.com
pietari.posti@gmail.com
140 GIANTS! Niña - Poster, 2008
141 Helsinki Design Week - Magazine Cover, 2008 | Client: Helsinki Design Week
142 GIANTS! Stained Polar Bear - Poster, 2008
143 GIANTS! Pulpo - Poster, 2008
144 Fashion meets Architecture - Editorial, 2008
145 Metropolis - Exhibition Poster, 2008 | Client: Now Showing Exhibition | Type Design by Underware
157 Escape - Book Illustration, 2008 | Client: Semipermanent Book 2008
160 The Beginning - Editorial, 2007 | Client: The New Scientist

Public Domain
USA
www.publicdomaindesign.com
info@publicdomaindesign.com
89 Islands - Poster, 2006 | Client: Satellite Ballroom
106 Neko Case - Poster, 2006 | Client: Starr Hill
116 Dungen - Poster, 2007 | Client: Black Cat DC
134 Rogue Wave, Wilco, Modest Mouse - Posters, 2007/2008 | Client: Charlottesville Pavilion
136 Broken Social Scene - Poster, 2008 | Client: Toad's Place Richmond
138 Wilco, Rogue Wave - Poster, 2006/2007 | Client: Charlottesville Pavilion
152 New Pornographers - Poster, 2008 | Client: Toad's Place Richmond
Designer: Matt Pamer

Rob Morris
Australia
www.digitalmash.com
rob@digitalmash.com
99 Piece & Love - Poster, 2009

Rülô
Chile
ruli-blume.blogspot.com
rulo.rulo.rulo.rulo@gmail.com
14 Caged-Ones - Poster, 2009 Credits: Andrea Dieterich
15 Diverse - Notebook Covers. 2008

Scotty Reifsnyder
USA
www.seescotty.com
scotty@seescotty.com
146 Young at Heart: Kinky Cat - Poster, 2007
147 Young at Heart: Rugged Stud - Poster, 2007
148 Young at Heart: White Rabbit - Poster, 2007
149 Don Peris Holiday Show - Poster, 2008 Client: Musician Don Peris
150/151 Johnny Cash: The Man Who Couldn't Cry - Children's Book, 2008
152 MFA show - Poster, 2007

Sellout Industries
Germany
www.sellout-industries.org
post@sellout-industries.org
36 Letterism - Textile Design, 2008
48 Painter - Textile Design, 2008
Faces - Textile Design, 2009 | Client: Adidas
Factory - Editorial 2009 | Client: Montana Spray Cans / Inflamamble Gmbh
49 Birds - Wrapping paper, 2008 Client: Beyond Fashion
Flowers - Textile Design, 2008 Client: Adidas Performance
76 Stuff Like That - Textile Design, 2009

Seripop
Canada
www.seripop.com
info@seripop.com
164 Art Pop Festival - Poster, 2006 | Client: Pop Montreal
165 Gothik Thursday - Flyer, 2008 | Client: Les Éditions de la Pastèque

Siggi Odds
Iceland
www.siggiodds.com
s@siggiodds.com
68 London Airwaves - Poster, 2008 | Client: Mr. Destiny
158 Lundi/Puffin - Personal 2008
159 Northwest Coast Self Portrait, Nang Jáadaas Exhibition - Art Prints, 2008

Silent Giant
USA
http://thesilentgiants.com/blog/
chris@thesilentgiants.com
97 Mogwai, Murder Death - Posters, 2008 | Client: The Crofoot Pontiac MI
36 Ra Ra Riot - Single & Album Cover, 2008/2009 | Client: Barsuk Records
103 Iron & Wine - Poster, 2008
110 Bon Iver - Poster, 2008 | Client: The Crofoot Pontiac MI
Designer: Christopher Everhart &/or Edward Knight

Skinny Laminx
South Africa
www.skinnylaminx.info
heather@skinnylaminx.com
33 Mountain Garden, 2008
77 Lava - Textile Design, 2008
78 Paper Cuts - 2008
Designer: Heather Moore

Spikepress
USA
www.spikepress.com
www.spikepress.com
41 The National Fake Empire - Poster, 2008 Client: The National
90 Chicago Jazz Fest 2008 - Poster, 2008 Client: Poster Plus
97 Devendra Banhart - Poster, 2004 Client: MP Shows
133 The National - Poster, 2008

Standard Design
USA
www.standard-design.com
tom@standard-design.com
153 No-Shadow Kick - Record Sleeve, 2005 Design: Tom Pappalardo

Strawberryluna
USA
www.strawberryluna.com
strawberryluna@strawberryluna.com
94 The Dirtbombs - Poster, 2007
113 The Detroit Cobras, Stars - Posters, 2007/2008
122 Spoon - Poster, 2007
123 Winter - Art Print, 2008
124 Spoon - Poster, 2007 | Client: The Electric Factory
125 The Dandy Warhols - Poster, 2008

Tad Carpenter
USA
www.tadcarpenter.com
tad@tadcarpenter.com
34 The Kooks - Poster, 2008 | Client: Myspace Secret Shows
45 My Morning Jacket - Poster, 2008 | Client: Eleven Production
93 Sigur Ros - Poster, 2008 | Client: Mammoth
102 Beck with MGMT - Poster, 2008 | Client: Eleven Production
104 Flatstock 17 - Poster, 2008
131 Fun Time - Art Print, 2008
130 Lovely - Art Print, 2008. This was created based on a drawing created by Vietnam orphan. Then sold to help that orphanage. | Client: Vietnam orphanages relief auction
Art Direction: Tad Carpenter and Dan Padavic/Vahalla Studios

Tes One
USA
www.tesone.net
info@tesone.net
86 Danny - Art Print, 2008
110 Open Season, Dog Friendly - Art Prints, 2009

The Heads of State
USA
www.theheadsofstate.com
info@theheadsofstate.com
36 The State of Social Media - Editorial, 2007 | Convene Magazine
86/87/ Obama's New Deal: Let's Innovate, Rebuild
93 America, Health Care We Can Afford, Educate for Growth - Editorial, 2009 | Client: New York Times | Illustrator: Dustin Summers | Art Director: Dustin Summers, Jason Kernevich, Cathy Gilmore-Barnes
87 NY Times Magazine - Magazine Cover, 2009
92 Portland International Film Festival - Poster, 2008
119 Green States - Editorial, 2008 | Client: Audubon Magazine
132 Fistful of Dollars - Poster, 2008 | Client: Rolling Roadshow | Designer: Dustin Summers
133 Gomez - Poster, 2007 | Designer: Dustin Summers Art Direction: Dustin Summers, Jason Kernevich

Todd Slater
USA
www.toddslater.net
slater.todd@gmail.com
44 Bright Eyes - Poster, 2007 | Client: Charles Attal Presents
46 Ween - Poster, 2007
87 The Starting Line - Poster, 2006 | Client: Live Nation
112 Good Charlotte - Poster, 2006 | Client: Live Nation
126 Of Montreal - Poster, 2007 | Client: Warehouse Live Jack Johnson - Poster, 2007 | Client: Live Nation
127 The Decemberists - Poster, 2007 | Client: Richard Goodall Gallery
135 Ween - Poster, 2007

Viola Welker
Germany
www.viola-welker.de
viola@viola-welker.de
35 Podencos - Paintings, 2008

Yehrin Tong
United Kingdom
http://yehrin.proteinos.com/fashion/index.html
yehrintong@hotmail.co.uk
28 Owl - Textile Design, 2005 | Client: Naughty Holdings Ltd.
29 Snake, Tiger, Mermaid - Textile Design, 2005 | Client: Maharishi

NAÏVE

MODERNISM AND FOLKLORE IN CONTEMPORARY GRAPHIC DESIGN

Edited by Robert Klanten & Hendrik Hellige.

Cover Illustration by Pietari Posti
Layout by Hendrik Hellige for Gestalten
Typeface: Generell TW by Michael Mischler
Foundry: www.gestalten.com/fonts

Project Management by Julian Sorge for Gestalten
Production Management by Martin Bretschneider for Gestalten
Printed by Artes Graficas Palermo, S.L., Madrid
Made in Europe

Published by Gestalten, Berlin 2009
ISBN 978-3-89955-247-8

For more information, please check www.gestalten.com

Bibliographic information published by the Deutsche Nationalbibliothek.
The Deutsche Nationalbibliothek lists this publication in the Deutsche Nationalbibliografie; detailed bibliographic data is available on the internet at http://dnb.d-nb.de.

None of the content in this book was published in exchange for payment by commercial parties or designers; Gestalten selected all included work based solely on its artistic merit.

This book was printed according to the internationally accepted FSC and ISO 14001 standards for environmental protection, which specify requirements for an environmental management system.

Gestalten is a climate neutral company and so are our products. We collaborate with the non-profit carbon offset provider myclimate (www.myclimate.org) to neutralize the company's carbon footprint produced through our worldwide business activities by investing in projects that reduce CO_2 emissions (www.gestalten.com/myclimate).